KIRBY

CHARLOTTE BROWNE

ULTIMATE FOOTBALL HEROES

KIRBY

FROM THE PLAYGROUND TO THE PITCH

DINO

Published by Dino Books,
an imprint of John Blake Publishing,
The Plaza,
535 Kings Road,
Chelsea Harbour,
London SW10 0SZ

www.johnblakebooks.com

www.facebook.com/johnblakebooks
twitter.com/jblakebooks

First published in paperback in 2019

ISBN: 978 1 78946 109 1

British Library Cataloguing-in-Publication Data:

A catalogue record for this book is available from the British Library.

Design by www.envydesign.co.uk

Printed and bound in Great Britain by Clays Ltd, Elcograf S.p.A.

1 3 5 7 9 10 8 6 4 2

John Blake Publishing is an imprint of Bonnier Books UK
www.bonnierbooks.co.uk

To my niece Heidi,
for showing me where the speed button
is on YouTube!

ULTIMATE FOOTBALL HEROES

Charlotte Browne knew from a young age she would probably end up working with words. She has worked as a journalist for a number of publications, from *The Independent* to *Prima*, and written for organisations within the not-for-profit and charity sectors. She is probably at her happiest walking in the Cornish countryside, swimming in the sea or playing her favourite songs on piano. She lives in south London.

Cover illustration by Dan Leydon.
To learn more about Dan visit danleydon.com
To purchase his artwork visit etsy.com/shop/footynews
Or just follow him on Twitter @danleydon

CONTENTS

CHAPTER 1

THE MOVE SOUTH

'Well, it's alright,' said Stephen Kirby, sighing deeply. 'It's hardly the Pennine mountain though, is it?'

His wife Denise laughed. 'Oh Stephen, come on, it's an area of outstanding beauty!'

'Yeah, so they might say down here, Deni, but they haven't seen what we grew up around, have they, eh?'

Stephen put his arm around his wife. They were looking out across the sweeping Chiltern Hills, a short drive, not far from their home on the outskirts of Reading. Their two small children Frances and James were with them.

It had been several years since the Kirbys had made the move south from Sunderland near Tyne and Wear to Berkshire. Since then Stephen had been working night shifts with Great Western Railway, the train company. Also, Deni worked as a nurse in a nearby hospital, so this was a rare day out for them all to enjoy as a family.

'You don't regret moving, do you?' Deni asked her husband.

'What, giving up what would have been a dazzling career with Sunderland Academy?' Stephen replied with a twinkle in his eye.

Deni snorted again. 'Oh, Stephen!'

'Don't laugh! If it hadn't been for that blasted injury I'd have sent Sunderland AFC soaring up into the Premier League! Or back to our good old former glory days of '36 at least!'

She patted him on the arm. 'I'm sorry, pet, I know how much football means to you.'

'It's okay. Nah, really don't regret it. Well, you know, course I miss the river Wear. Oh, the walks along there...'

'We have the Thames!'

'Pah!'

She smiled. 'And of course, our families back home.'

'Yeah, I miss them too.' They were both silent for a moment, contemplating.

'Well, obviously I moved down here to get away from your family!'

'Oh Stephen!'

'You wouldn't get them moving down here to live with a load of southerners.'

She chuckled. 'They still look a bit puzzled when I call you "pet"!'

'I know!'

'Strange to think, our children aren't going to grow up with Geordie accents.'

'Not if I can help it!'

They looked over at their two children, Frances and James, who were playing with a football. At four and three years old respectively, barely a year between them, for the most part they played sweetly with each other. Unless a football was involved. Then gentle play often turned to outright war as they both tried to gain control of it.

'James!' Deni cried, as he tackled his younger sister to the floor. 'Careful!'

'Ah, it's in the genes,' said Stephen proudly. 'Destiny.' He actively encouraged his children's love of the sport and had taken them to a few Sunderland games already that year.

'I'll make sure I pass the mantle of greatness on to my son that's for sure,' he added.

Deni laughed. 'Oh go away with you, Stephen! Although I wouldn't underestimate your daughter's talents either!'

'No,' he said thoughtfully, 'you're right.'

They both looked on as Fran, undeterred, was back off the ground, chasing enthusiastically after her brother who was heading off down the hill. She was tiny, even for her age group, but fast on her feet and sturdy.

'Go on, Frances! Go on!' her dad encouraged. She caught her brother up, kicked the ball away from him and began to dribble it.

'See!' said Deni. 'She's quite something.'

'Natural instinct already! See – it's in the genes!'

Deni laughed. 'Well, it looks as though we might have a proper pair of football stars on our hands to coach!'

'Yeah, as long as they support Sunderland! Not Reading... heaven forbid.'

'Well at least Reading are in the First Division!'

They both laughed as they continued to stroll through the countryside and snap photos of the pair battling it out for the ball.

'We'll have to send some photos back home,' said Deni.

'*Forever my Sunderland, I will stand by you... my blood runs red and white...*'

'Oh don't sing, Stephen, it sounds bad!'

CHAPTER 2

WATCHING THIERRY

'Hai-yah – Judo chop!'

'What the?!' Stephen cried out as Fran jumped from out of a tree in their garden, landing on his back.

'Flipping 'eck!'

Deni came running out of the back door to catch sight of Fran chopping her little hand at her dad.

'Hai – ya!' She cried, thrusting her leg out towards him.

'Come on, Dad – at least *try* and block me!'

He started laughing. 'We didn't send you to judo lessons so that you could attack your own dad, you know – besides, kicks and chops are Karate, not Judo!'

She giggled. 'Resistance is futile, Dad!'

Fran was seven years old and one of the smallest in her year. Her parents had decided to send her to judo classes to ensure her height didn't affect her confidence. It appeared to be working, and she seemed happy to spar with anyone, regardless of their size.

'Okay, Dad, let's play football. I'm bored of beating you at judo.'

Deni watched as her daughter keepie-uppied with a football and began to dribble it down the garden. She marvelled at Fran's boundless energy, speed and athleticism in all her sporting activities. But it was notable that, when the girl had a ball at her feet, a huge smile spread out across her face and her big brown eyes began to twinkle.

Fran was especially fired up when she was wearing her favourite Number 14 Arsenal away strip and pretending to be her hero Thierry Henry. She recorded *Match of the Day* clips of Arsenal's new signing and endlessly replayed them, so that she could study his moves and learn all the tricks.

Still dribbling, Fran reached her dad, who was

stuck in the middle of a makeshift goal cobbled together from old flowerpots.

She chattered to herself, pretending to take on opponents: 'And here he comes! He's in the middle! Cool as a cucumber! He takes on one, then another – and another! He's in the penalty box! Is he gonna shoot from there? He makes it look so easy! Get ready, Dad!'

She warned Stephen as she took aim with her left boot. 'And it is so easy! He scores!'

Her father fell to the ground as he attempted to save her shot.

'Great left boot, pet,' he said, 'but you've got to make sure your right is just as strong, we need to do some work on that.' Already, her father was one of her toughest critics.

Her mother called out: 'That's a Thierry Henry finish, Frances! Very cool!'

Her father got up, dusting himself down. He groaned. 'Ah, I dunno, why do you have to be an Arsenal fan?'

'Because I'm a Thierry Henry fan, Dad – he's amazing!'

'Now let me tell you about Sunderland's player, Mickey...'

'Oh Dad. I don't care! No-one plays like Henry on the field! I wanna play like him one day!' Already at seven, Fran could identify her idol's ability on both the wing and as a lone striker, that could easily take on players one on one.

'You will play like him!' her mum called out from the kitchen. 'Better than him! Arsenal will want you in no time!'

'Sunderland!' her dad protested.

'Mmm, Mum,' said Fran. 'Are you cooking what I think you're cooking? Smells delicious!'

'That's right, enchiladas, your favourite!'

'When I grow up, Mum, all I'm ever going to eat is enchiladas! They're the best!'

'Hmm, I don't know if you can survive on enchiladas alone!'

'I don't care, Mum – I'm going to eat so many I'll turn into an enchilada!'

'I'll have to teach you how to make them properly.'

'Or you can just make them for me forever!'

Deni laughed as Fran ran inside and threw her arms around her. She looked into her daughter's eyes that sparkled from underneath a wave of blonde hair. Deni had long given up trying to tame or comb it. There wasn't much point – she was always out playing.

Fran grabbed her favourite enchilada – avocado with Mexican bean – and began to wolf it down.

'Frances! What's the hurry?'

'James's mates are playing football down Caversham Park. I don't wanna miss them!'

James and his friends were only a year older than her, but they seemed like giants to Fran, as they were considerably taller than she was – not that she was fazed by that. She'd always wanted to play football to be cool, like them, tagging along to join in with their games in the park. But James never discouraged her. Neither did any of his friends – if they objected, they were soon silenced when they found out how nifty she was on her feet.

The doorbell rang. James stumbled down the stairs

to answer, but not before grabbing an enchilada for himself.

'Alright, sis! You ready?'

'You'll look after your sister, eh?' said Deni.

'She can look after herself!'

Fran nodded at her mum proudly. James turned to his friends, friends that Fran didn't recognise, and said: 'My sister's coming too – that alright?'

She saw them both pull a bit of a face in surprise and she smiled to herself.

'Just you wait,' she thought. Fran loved it when her brother brought friends she hadn't played with before. It was a chance to show them what she could do.

As Deni watched her daughter run off she turned to her husband. 'You know – I never see her happier than when she's about to play football. She absolutely whizzed out of that door.'

'She's very athletic, loves lots of sports.'

'She is. But I never see her eyes light up more than when she's got a ball at her feet. I think football's the sport we should really encourage her in.'

'You think she could really go far?'

'I *know*, Stephen. She's got real talent. I think she could make it.'

'I knew living south would get to you one day, love.'

'Oh, Stephen!'

CHAPTER 3

ROYALS SEAL OF APPROVAL

The park was only a short distance away. As soon as they got there Fran broke out into a run, feeling the wind in her hair. James's friends looked surprised as she ran past them. She smiled and waved. She loved coming here on a Sunday to practise, with all the other kids up on the common, which boasted beautiful views across the hills.

Fran started to commandeer her brother and his friends. 'Hey, if we can get a few others to play over there, we could have enough for a five-a-side. Bagsy me striker!'

'Hang on, Fran,' said her brother. 'We're actually

down here to do some training and play a game on the pitch.'

'Oh yeah? Who with?'

'Some coaches from the Royals.'

'What? *The* Royals? As in Reading FC?'

She looked over the heath and saw a group of adults walking towards them in the famous blue-and-white-striped home kit. James's friends turned to her with a serious look on their faces, arms folded.

'Yeah, they might be scouting from Reading FC. It's a pretty big deal. They're starting training here on Sundays, looking for people they might want to play in the junior teams.'

'Great!' replied Fran. She looked at her brother.

One of the coaches approached them. 'Right, is this everyone?'

'Can I take part, please?' Fran implored.

'Have you registered?'

'No. But please can I just play one game?' Fran looked at the group of boys. Not one girl among them and they were all taller and bigger than her. This would be interesting.

'Okay, just one!'

Fran beamed, but not everyone was pleased. She heard some of the boys tut and moan under their breaths, and they looked clearly annoyed.

'Well, she does look a bit like a boy with her short hair,' one of them quipped.

'Ha!' said another. 'What's with your funny voice?'

Much to her dad's delight, Fran had picked up a Geordie accent from her parents. She was losing it at school, although it remained strong enough for other kids to pick up on. But most of the time she was just called 'that little Geordie Fran' good-naturedly.

On this occasion, though, her face fell a little. She was used to a bit of teasing from her brother and his friends sometimes, but this reference to her accent felt a bit malicious.

'I'm from Newcastle – idiot!' she shouted back.

I'll show them, she thought. She was now determined to prove them wrong.

There were more than enough players for an eleven-a-side. Fran had worked out early on that she enjoyed getting up front and on the attack, but as long as she had opportunities to run about on the field she was in her element.

'This should be easy,' she heard someone mutter, just before the whistle blew. The hostile stares and sniggers lingered. Still, James was on the same team as her, so she felt she had some support from her sibling. He looked over at her and smiled. He knew what she was capable of.

If a bit of doubt crept in, she thought of her mum saying: 'Arsenal will want you one day. You're as good as Henry!' A big smile broke out on her face, and she scaled the field, scanning for different routes in to attack. The whistle blew and she felt her feet take off down the pitch towards the penalty area. She was well aware that she was short but it gave her a good centre of gravity and great balance.

She heard the lads shouting to each other as she looked for opportunities to get hold of the ball: 'Pass to me!' 'Pass to me!'

She saw a clear space open up that she could run into as one of her teammates reached the penalty area. He paid no attention.

'I'll have to put more pressure on attack,' she thought to herself. Then a chance opened up for her on the left flank. One of the opposition lost possession of the ball, and she took the opportunity to tear after it. Once she'd caught up and made contact with it, she dribbled speedily towards the goal.

She then wound her way around two defenders who tried to encircle her, instinctively turning this way and that, shielding the ball with her entire body. Once she'd broken through them, she continued down on the left side. There was a team player to her right that she could pass to but, as she got inside the penalty area, she managed to cut inside a defender trying to block her. Her feet moved nimbly and deftly – and in a moment of pure bravado she looked into the eyes of the goalkeeper (a trick Thierry recommended), before she shot low into the net.

GOAL!

She'd scored within fifteen minutes of the first half. Joy swept over her as she heard her whole team cheer, and as she felt her brother pat her on the back.

'Well done, sis!' he said.

She played on, running rings all around the opposition, navigating her way round defenders and blocking attacks in midfield. They conceded only one goal and she went on to score two more.

During the game, Fran sensed the atmosphere on the pitch towards her change, from one of hostility to respect. Some of the boys who'd sniggered or laughed were looking at her differently. She didn't really have any female friends that she'd played football with – not yet anyway. But she knew in her own little way she'd made a difference there today. She'd proved herself. And they might think twice before they assumed another girl couldn't play football.

The coach walked towards her.

'What's your name again?' he said.

'Frances! Well, my mum calls me Frances but I prefer Fran.' Her Geordie lilt rang out across the pitch.

'Well, Fran.' He took her aside. 'You silenced your critics, eh?'

She smiled.

'I think you should try out for the Royals,' he went on.

'Really?'

'Yes, one of the junior teams at Reading FC. We're holding trials for our Under-10s team next weekend. You'd be training twice a week and playing a fixture at the weekends.'

He added, with a twinkle in his eye: 'You would be in a girls' team, though, would you mind?'

Fran shrugged. The thought of playing with girls did seem a bit alien to her but she could probably get used to it.

'Don't worry, though,' he said. 'You'll play in the East Berkshire Football Alliance Boys League each season. So, you'll get a chance to pulverise them again.'

Fran beamed from ear to ear. She couldn't wait to go home and tell her mum and dad.

CHAPTER 4

TAKING ACTION

'Okay, I've cooked you some pasta, pet – a lovely carbohydrate to keep you going throughout training!'

Deni was in the kitchen busy making pasta for Fran. After a long shift as a nurse at the hospital she always made sure she was home at five to take Fran to after-school training. Deni also drove her to training twice a week and at the weekends. She'd sit in the car for two hours waiting for her whatever the weather – rain, snow or sun. When it was cold her mum would have a hot flask of cocoa waiting for her as a 'treat' and warm an extra pair of gloves up for her.

Fran sloped into the kitchen with her dressing gown on. She looked at her mum hurriedly preparing dinner for her. She'd also packed her *101 Dalmatians* lunchbox on the side, all ready with snacks for breaks during training. Fran loved Disney films. Every year her mum saved up so that they could go to Disneyland together – it was their annual treat and Fran loved every minute they spent together.

In short, Deni was utterly supportive as a parent. But this is why Fran did not feel good about the lie she was about to tell now.

She coughed. Her mum looked up and saw her in her dressing gown. Puzzled, she asked sharply: 'Why aren't you in your kit?'

'I don't feel well, Mum.'

Deni walked over and felt her temperature. 'Come on Fran, there's nought wrong with you, what's this about? We need to go soon!'

'Aaww, Mum, I just don't feel like it!

'Don't feel like it? Don't feel like it! There are plenty of things we don't always feel like doing in our lives. Your dad and I don't always feel like going out and working each day but we do. But I know you. And I know you love football. You've been given a great opportunity to play for the Royals and I'm not sitting by and seeing you squander this precious talent. So tell me what's up – or get in the car!'

Fran knew her mum was no pushover, and it wouldn't be an easy fight. She was going to have to admit some truths.

'I just... it's not fun anymore...'

'Why?'

She blurted out: 'They're all, they're all so much bigger than me!'

She then burst into tears.

Her mum went over and gave her a big hug.

'I didn't think that ever bothered you. Is someone picking on you?'

She shook her head. 'I don't like being the titchy one all the time. Some of the ten-year-old girls are enormous, Mum!'

'Oh, sweetheart, I know... but you won't *always* be the "titchy one". You'll grow and it will all level out. And think of all those smaller players – Romário... Pelé... Baixinho. They're not even really that much taller than you! See how far they got!

If anything, their size was a blessing – great things come in small packages!'

Fran smiled through frustrated tears.

Deni sighed. 'You really are perfect as you are. What you lack in height I know you make up for in different ways. You're fast, tenacious, have great dexterity, deft and you're a quick thinker on the pitch.'

'When they let me on the pitch...'

'What?'

'The coach keeps putting me in goal. He says my height's an advantage because I can go for those low shots. But I can't keep anything out – it's embarrassing!'

'Well, no wonder you're so miserable – you're meant to be out there on the pitch moving around! Why did he decide to put you in there?'

Fran shrugged.

'Hmm, right,' said Deni. 'I'm going to have a word.'

Fran smiled through the tears. Things always seemed to get sorted whenever Mum 'had a word'.

Though she also immediately felt a bit sorry for her coach who'd be on the receiving end of her mum's scolding.

'But you know what, Fran. You have to remember that you're also a team. You all have different strengths and weaknesses that work well as a whole together.'

'I guess so, Mum.'

'Fran, listen to me, you're going to play for England one day.'

'Do you really think so, Mum?'

'I know it. You're the best player in the world.'

'You believe that?'

'Would I say it every single day if I didn't?'

She gave her a big hug.

'Now, young lady, Pelé didn't get where he did today moping about in a dressing gown – get into the car! Dreams don't happen without action – you've got to go and live them!'

CHAPTER 5

KELLY AND HARRIET

As it turned out, there was no need for Deni to 'have a word' that night. When they arrived at Hogwood Park Training Ground, Fran discovered the team had a new coach.

Fran was immediately struck by how young and bubbly she was. She had blonde hair and a warm, welcoming smile.

'Hello everybody! I'm Kelly Chambers. I'm really looking forward to working with you and I'm hoping to learn just as much from you as you are from me.'

She added: 'It wasn't so long ago that I was in your shoes, in the Under-10s team, right here on these very grounds. This team is incredibly dear to me and I can't wait to see you all develop as players.'

Fran was very happy to have the chance to run about more on the pitch. It was definitely where she felt more at home. She thought about what her mum said as she played too. It was true. Yes they were taller, bigger and older – but not necessarily better. Just different. And they could all work together as a team. As her attitude towards it changed, she felt her confidence grow on the pitch, and realised that the older girls took more notice of her.

Her new coach noticed too. At the end of training, she pulled Fran aside: 'You must have been quite frustrated in goal, eh?'

Fran nodded.

'Great dribbling, Fran,' she added. 'I think we can work on making your finishing more decisive and improve your passing. But I think there's an exciting player in you.'

Then Kelly addressed the whole team:

'I'm really pleased with how you're all playing. I think with a bit more work and training, we'll be ready to take on some of our first opponents of the season!'

The girls cheered.

Fran had noticed a new girl at training that night too. As was the norm, the newcomer was taller than her, but Fran guessed she was about the same age. She had blonde hair and kind blue eyes. They smiled shyly at each other after the game and walked back towards the car park where parents were collecting their kids.

The girl spoke to her. 'Are you Superwoman?'

Fran laughed.

'Sorry, that was a silly joke!' said the girl. 'But you are fast!'

'Thanks!'

'You're new to this club then?'

'Yeah, we just moved. Dad's gutted of course 'cause the football team aren't that great!'

They both laughed.

'Yes,' said the girl. 'But you just want to play football!'

'Yeah,' smiled Fran. 'It's funny. My dad can't get over me not playing for Sunderland.'

'Is that where you're from? I thought you had a bit of an accent!'

'Yeah, but whenever I go back home they say I sound southern!'

'Can't win!', laughed Harriet. 'What school do you go to?'

'I'm going to start at Caversham Park soon.'

'Oh yeah? That's my school. Maybe we'll be in the same class.'

'Same footie team, same class, we'd better get on!'

They both laughed.

'I'm Harriet, by the way.'

'Fran.'

As they waved each other goodbye, Fran somehow had the sense they'd end up knowing each other for a long time to come.

On the way back home in the car, Fran felt a weight lift from her shoulders. She was glad that she'd discussed how she felt with her mum. And she was so happy with the new coach. And her potential new friend. Her mum looked over to her and smiled as she turned up the volume on one of her favourite, most carefree tunes – and they both sang it at the top of their voices together.

CHAPTER 6

FACING THE RENEGADES

'Okay, girls, let's show them what we're made of then!'

Fran's heart soared as she strode out with the rest of the John Madejski Academy (JMA) team into the stadium. She turned to smile at Harriet, who was walking along beside her.

They were both beaming with pride to be wearing the blue-and-white striped kit. The night before they'd painted their toenails together in the club colours to pay homage to their first-ever match of the season against the Reading Renegades. The entire team gasped as they took in the size of the John Madejski Stadium.

'This is amazing!'

'We've finally arrived, girls!'

It was their first time playing at the home ground of Reading FC and the 24,000 capacity filled them with nerves and delight. This was quite a contrast, compared to their previous games, with their families cheering them on from the sidelines of some football pitch, huddling in waterproofs, trying to stay warm. Deni always turned up whatever the weather but Fran was pleased to think she was shielded this time under the roof. Of course, they were nowhere near to filling the capacity but they had enough friends and families in the crowd to support them. She could already hear her mum cheering on the team.

Fran looked round at the smiling faces of her eleven-a-side team. They'd all been working hard for this opportunity and were looking forward to playing in the league. Over the past few years Kelly Chambers had been working hard with all the players to hone their individual skills and qualities. Under her tuition Fran was developing her skills as a left winger and building up her strength in both her left and right feet, so that she was just as effective on either wing. She was also developing her ability to pick up passes, take crosses and score at close range. And she was becoming more confident at taking on opponents and attempting more shots on goal.

'We'll make a great striker out of you yet, Fran!' said Kelly.

Ultimately, Fran knew she wanted to play in that position because it seemed to be the most creative, the one where she could express herself the most. But there were many other decent strikers in the team who were, not surprisingly, taller than her. However, it was just a matter of time and Fran knew that, under Kelly's tutelage, she would continue to thrive.

Up until now, the girls had only played against girls though. Their match against Reading Renegades was the first time they'd played against boys.

Fran remembered all the times she'd played against boys when she was younger and was surprised to find herself feeling a little nervous about it.

Kelly reassured them. 'You girls are a much

stronger force of nature to contend with, I can promise you.'

Fran looked across at the strikers Polly and Sally, then Harriet, who was developing into a formidable defender under Kelly's guidance too. It was true. They were a strong unit.

'If they're tougher and stronger, they'll make us tougher and stronger! We don't want to be playing weaker players!' Kelly continued to rally the girls.

But as they walked out onto the pitch, she felt her heart skip a beat as she heard old familiar jeers and snorts from the team, taunts she'd not heard in a while.

'Ha ha, look – here comes the knitting class,' said one male voice.

'Where are your Barbie dolls, girls?'

'Now, now lads,' said their coach as Kelly gave them all a stern look.

'We're just teasing, sir. Can't they take it?!'

But then another said: 'Well, if girls were that good, why aren't there any proper teams? They don't even have a proper league!'

Fran had to admit he had a point. There was no professional women's league in the UK and although she was still very young, she wondered how possible it was to build a career out of it, despite all her mum's encouragement. When she turned on the TV she didn't see any female football stars playing, and none of her role models were women. She had watched the Women's World Cup in '99 with huge excitement and hoped something like that could happen in the UK.

But maybe it was true, maybe they were all kidding themselves. What future was there for her in football?

But then The Royals all turned to each other and smiled with a look that said: 'Let's show them. The boys won't squash our spirits!'

Kelly turned to them all and gave them a huge smile. 'Come on girls – you can do this! Prove them wrong!'

But as the whistle blew and they started playing, Fran felt that something wasn't quite gelling between them all. Her team were losing a few opportunities to get control of the ball in midfield and she could see the defenders were being pushed to the limits. She also had a particularly strong marker who was constantly on her heels.

As they neared the end of the first half, they still hadn't scored. But they hadn't conceded either.

What would Thierry Henry do? Fran thought of his ability to get past opponents with pace, technical skill and composure. 'Get hold of that ball, get yourself into the penalty area and run with it towards goal.' She ran through his classic moves in her head and thought of all she'd practised in training on her finishing – shooting right with the left inside of her foot into the far right corner of the goal.

In the middle of the field Fran picked up the ball. She ran as fast as she could down the left wing. She felt most comfortable there as she could use her left foot for leverage and dribble at speed.

If you get a chance, take your time, she told herself. She heard the crowd cheer as she flew forward at pace towards the penalty area, putting all her focus into keeping close contact with the ball, trusting that her feet would know where to go. She slowed down as she met with her first defender to put him off, then picked up her pace again and cut on the inside past him. She smiled to herself as she successfully outfoxed him and ran on. She was now in the penalty box. Time to head for the goal! Keep the ball close, and don't think too much, she told herself. She saw the goalkeeper was agitated, as he came out towards her and tried to anticipate her move.

Finish now, Fran! Finish how you want! Finish with speed. Go for it! She looked in the goalkeeper's eyes. They were dismissive, mean, unkind. Their look distracted her. She hesitated. She realised she'd given it too long. She'd lost the momentum and fluidity in her movements.

She shot anyway. It went wide. Very wide. She shook her fists with frustration as she saw it soar to the right of the net.

As she crashed to the ground, she slid in the mud and her left foot went up into the air. As she lay on her back she felt humiliated as well as angry with herself. She was so fed up she almost didn't want to get up.

She heard the laughter start. A player from the other team ran past and cried: 'Now that's why they don't have a woman's league – ha ha!'

'Stick to hairdressing, love!'

Fran slammed her fist into the mud, her hair falling over her eyes. Her left thigh and knee hurt. She hated making a mistake or messing up, least of all in front of the boys. She wished she could just slide back into the mud and pretend the embarrassment had never happened.

CHAPTER 7

SEE IT AND BELIEVE IT!

'Come on, Fran!' she heard one of her teammates yell. 'You've got to get back up! You've got to play on!'

Harriet came rushing over to see if she was alright. She held out her arm. 'Don't let them see they've got to you, Fran!'

But they *had* got to her. A few more of her teammates ran over. This was always the way. Because she was small she felt extra pressure to show she was able to get up and carry on. She knew they were doing it to try and bolster her, but it left her feeling angrier in that moment and as though she was the pathetic, timid weak link of the team.

Then her determination returned. 'Alright, alright!' she said, getting to her feet.

Kelly came running over. 'Are you alright, Fran?'

'Yes, I'm fine.'

'You sure?'

In truth, her knee was still hurting a little but it was the mistake that hurt more now. Whenever she made an error, it threw her off course and her concentration was affected for the rest of the game. She kept replaying the moment in her mind, going over what she should have done instead. Her teammate Polly scored after half-time, but the opposing Renegades went on to win 3–1. Fran felt as though she'd let the whole team down and couldn't stop beating herself up.

'Don't worry, Fran,' said Harriet, putting her arm round her. 'That was a really good shot you tried.'

'I know. It's really annoying. I should have played better.'

'Oh don't be daft Fran, we're a team – remember?'

Kelly consoled the girls. 'They had stronger, more experienced attackers. It wasn't meant to be for us this time. But we'll be back. And we'll beat them next time.'

She also took Fran aside and said: 'It's okay to make mistakes on the pitch. We all do. It's how you deal with them and learn from them that counts.'

'I messed up, miss. Pure and simple. They were better. I'm rubbish.'

'Well yes, today they were better. But I think something went on with your head, Fran. You let the mistake get all bigger and uglier than it should be – you let it become a big scary monster! Don't let it!'

'That's the problem,' Fran said with a smile. 'Everyone is bigger than me!'

'Well, it has its benefits...'

'If one more person tells me that!' replied Fran.

'Well, there's not as far to get up when you fall down!'

They both laughed.

'That's more like it!' said Kelly.

'Now, this might cheer you up some more. We're looking for players to take part in our Centre of

Excellence Programme and Player Development Programme.'

Fran's ears pricked up. She knew this was where some of the strongest players in the club had been nurtured. It was part of the FA Girls' England Talent Pathway scheme, which aimed to work with girls who had footballing potential. Many of them were tipped for England.

'It does mean more coaching, more training,' continued Kelly. 'But it's a lot more support. But it's not that long till you start your GCSEs. So if you want to do it you'll have to think about how to balance your studies and football more.'

Fran smiled, but she had a few doubts. 'Is there much point? No-one seems to take women's football that seriously.'

'Yes, well we're trying to change that and invest more in it. It is growing. We want to get as good as the German, US and Canadian teams. England didn't even qualify for the World Cup last year.'

She continued: 'Trouble is, it's barely advertised or televised. England has some great players like Kelly

Smith and others who aren't getting the exposure or even the development they deserve.'

Fran had recently watched footage of Kelly Smith playing in the 2005 European Championships and thought she was a great player.

'And we're losing great players to the US because there's no professional league. But this is going to change. I think we'll follow in these countries' footsteps eventually. Still, it's all relatively new. The last World Cup in 2003 was only the fourth one.'

Kelly concluded: 'But it's why developing players like you is so important to us.'

Fran blushed. After that day's game, it was great to hear this. Her dream of playing for England beckoned closer.

Her mum couldn't stop smiling when she heard the news.

'See?! I told you. Best player in the world!'

'Maybe one day, Mum.'

'No – see it and believe it now!'

CHAPTER 8

PRACTICE, PRACTICE, PRACTICE!

At the Centre of Excellence Academy, Kelly encouraged Fran to think further about what she wanted to get better at.

Fran thought for a moment, and replied: 'Being a really great goal scorer!'

'What do you need to work on, to be that?'

Fran knew there wasn't just one thing.

'Lots of things.'

'Can you break them down for me?'

'You need to be fast, have brilliant technique and positional awareness.'

'What do you mean by positional awareness?'

'I think... knowing where your team is going to be.'

'How will you get better at that?'

Fran sighed a little. 'Practice.'

'Indeed!' said Kelly. 'Practice, practice, practice! This is why we train! The more you train, the more ready and prepared you will be for every potential situation on the field. But what's the most important thing to remember about a successful striker?'

Fran thought about it. Eventually, she said, 'They're always striving to get better. They always want to improve. They don't ever switch off or get complacent.'

'Exactly! We can teach you what we know. But natural ability or "being special" will only get you so far. If you're prepared to put in the extra work and application we can make you a great player. And remember, that every single striker has taken hundreds of shots and missed many.'

Fran took on board everything that Kelly said. She went back to basics perfecting her dribbling skills even more, weaving in and out of cones in the garden, as her mum watched, cheering her on. Fran pretended the cones were defenders – or the lads from the Renegades. She learnt to slow down a little and practise her touches with both feet, prioritising movement over speed. The exercise really helped her and as her confidence grew she began to speed up.

She knew that she was fairly comfortable on her left foot so she worked on making her right foot just as strong. She practised adding curl and spin to her goals, her finishing and shots on target, over and over, until it began to feel more like second nature. She practised taking different positions on the field. Her shots on target began to feel less aimless as she perfected knowing exactly where they were going to go.

Kelly also worked with her to improve her Cruyff turn. Fran had always enjoyed this manoeuvre for its trickery – it meant she could get better at outfoxing her opponents as she cut in on the inside, and also improve how she shielded the ball with her body.

'You're small, which means you've a good centre of gravity.'

Fran groaned. 'Don't tell me – I can use it to my advantage!'

Kelly laughed. 'It's true. And the best players know it too. You can change direction with more strength and speed, which gives you the upper hand over your opponents, believe me. It's particularly effective for the shoulder drop too.'

'Shoulder drop?'

'This is another trick that will confuse opponents.' Kelly showed her how to balance her weight onto her right foot, as though she was about to lead in that direction, then cut in, on the opposite route.

'Your body seems to be doing one thing but your foot is doing something completely different!'

As time went on Kelly grew more impressed with Fran's attitude to training.

'You've been working so hard, Fran,' said Kelly one day. 'I can really see your improvement. But a goal scorer also needs to be able to read a game and react incredibly quickly. How do you think you can work on getting better at that?'

Fran smiled. 'Here comes the attitude speech.'

Kelly laughed. 'If you remain focused on the game – right up until the ninetieth minute – a lot of the skills and techniques will just fall into place. If you can clear your mind regardless of what's happened that day – whether it's a bad mark at school or an argument with your friend – that goal is just waiting to be scored. It may not be right until the end of the match. But it will come. So if you make any mistakes, what must you do?'

'Put them in the past, where they belong.'

Kelly nodded. 'And lastly, remember to be a generous player. There are times when you can pass that ball to your team player. Don't take all the glory.'

Fran knew she was developing as a player from the extra coaching and training, and she couldn't wait to get out and show off the skills she'd learnt and put them into practice.

CHAPTER 9

REVENGE

Fran's heart thumped as The Royals ran onto the pitch to once more face the Reading Renegades. But this time it wasn't thumping from nerves. It was from excitement.

The Royals were back at Madejski Stadium and Kelly had gathered them together for a pre-match pep talk, to make sure the venue didn't trigger any unpleasant memories.

'Put the last match behind you now and just go for the goal this time, girls. You've been creating some wonderful attacking opportunities. If we can keep that ball on the right side of the field I know Fran and Kate can make a difference up in the penalty area. Let's show those Renegades we mean business. We concede nothing!'

They all cheered.

'Okay – let's go!'

As they ran out onto the pitch the team heard sniggers from the opposition:

'Oh, hi girls – back again?'

'The Royals?'

'Right royal embarrassment, I'll say.'

'Not humiliated enough the first time round, were you?'

Fran, along with the rest of the team, turned to them and waved.

Fran's dad still worked a lot of night shifts and so wasn't present for the game, but her mum Deni and her brother James had brought a band of supporters for the match. Deni had made banners and knitted scarves, with all the Royals' team colours. James had even brought a banner which read: 'Go – our little Geordie Fran!'

From the outset of the game, JMA dominated. Fran's first chance came earlier than she expected as

Polly passed to her from midfield. Fran caught the ball on first touch outside the penalty box and started running down the right flank towards the penalty area. She picked up her pace as she ran and kept the ball as close to her as possible. Two defenders spotted the danger she presented and tore after her. But she was too quick for them.

Fran felt as though she'd never had as much fun in all her life as she made her way into the penalty box and faced more defenders. And she was happy to take her time. She paused for a moment, before she cut in on one defender and flew past them. Then she was on her own in the box. She saw the goalkeeper come out, anticipating that she'd kick to the right. She waited a second before he lunged in the wrong direction and then she nudged the ball delicately into the left of the net.

GOAL!

After that first goal, there was no stopping her. It felt as though the ball hardly left her foot as she darted in and out, tearing past defenders who desperately tried to chase her down. The first half flew by as they scored goal after goal. By half-time they were already six goals up, and they'd conceded none.

The Renegades were not happy and couldn't find a way back into the game, as much as they tried. They couldn't break down JMA's defence and during the second half began to unravel as a team, turning on each other and their downtrodden goalie. 'What's wrong with you?!' they all started to shout at each other.

In the stands angry-looking parents began to shake their fists and shout, as the cheers from JMA's supporters grew louder:

'Come on, lads!'

'You're not gonna get beaten by a bunch of little girls, are you?! Pull yourselves together!'

But as the final minutes of the match ticked by, the Renegades had no hope of clawing back. Fran, along with the other strikers, kept effortlessly scoring goals. In total, Fran scored an incredible nine goals, effectively three hat tricks. When the final whistle blew, the score was 13–0. The girls leapt around and cheered with Kelly as they celebrated their win.

'Now come on girls,' said Kelly with a twinkle in her eye, 'we must do the decent thing and shake hands with the opposition.' But the losing side were nowhere to be seen on the pitch. They were already heading for home – dejected, angry and in floods of tears.

CHAPTER 10

WHEN, NOT IF

Fran's gaze was glued to the TV screen, breaking only momentarily to take a bite out of an enchilada. She was watching the 2007 Women's World Cup unfold. BBC Two was showing live coverage of the tournament, which was taking place in China for the first time. It was England vs Argentina, and Fran was enthralled. It was the first time in twelve years that England had qualified and they were performing brilliantly through the group stages.

Fran, by now fourteen, was particularly captivated by Kelly Smith's two last-minute stellar goals against Japan in their last match, in order for England to equalise, but was equally impressed by England's young new midfielder, Jill Scott, who was blazing a trail in her first international tournament.

'GOAL!' Fran screamed as she leapt up in the air. 'That was terrific!' Scott had just scored her first against Argentina ten minutes into the game.

Her mum looked over, smiling. She was just as pleased that the BBC were televising the matches in China. Maybe the tide was changing in women's football. And it was a good sign that the English team were progressing with some fresh heroes for Fran's generation to look up to.

Fran looked at her excitedly. 'Mum – she's terrific. She's new but she's already making such a difference to the team – really shaking up the field of attack and everything.'

'Fara Williams is a great player too,' Fran continued. 'Plays for Everton. We need more players who are this good to be taken seriously. Then maybe they'll put a professional league together.'

'They deserve it,' said her mum, 'after the way they've played in this tournament.'

'Most of them are only playing in semi-professional teams, if that. They're all doing day jobs on the side, then squeezing in their training during the week. And still they're expected to play as well as if they were still doing it full-time!'

'No, it's not fair,' agreed her mum. 'I hope it's easier when you're playing professionally.'

'*When* I'm playing professionally?' smiled Fran, conscious that there was still no professional league for women in the UK.

'Well yes,' said Deni, 'it's a question of when, not if' – and she smiled back.

Fran knew she always had the unwavering support of her mum. Still only in her early teens, football remained an uncertain career possibility for her, but she'd given up judo to concentrate on it. She was still playing in the John Madejski Academy (for under-16s) and they didn't think it would be long until she made her debut for Reading FC.

School was still important to her and she knew many of England's best players kept studying alongside their football careers. But it gave her hope to see other women playing this well for England and being properly invested in. A career in football was beginning to look more possible, with or without a professional league.

'Mum, it won't be long till I can learn to drive. Then you won't have to drive me to all my training and games.'

'Well you'll have to get your own car, there's no way I'm letting you loose in mine!'

'Well if I make it big I'll buy a Bentley – just like that Wayne Rooney's!'

'Yes! And you can buy me a penthouse on Sandbanks too!'

They both laughed.

'One day, Mum.'

Her mum smiled. 'I think I'll miss it though anyway Fran, taking you to games.'

Fran looked back at the TV and all the England team in their blue-and-white kits as the whistle blew for the end of the game. They were all hugging each other and celebrating their 6–1 victory over Argentina. Under the guiding hand of their coach Hope Powell, they'd made a great comeback. Fran wanted to be part of a team like that, playing the sport she loved for her country.

CHAPTER 11

THE MEETING

'Jill! Jill!'

Fran jumped up and down excitedly. She was with a group of other fans who were queuing up outside Meadow Park at Borehamwood, home of Arsenal Ladies, all desperate to get a sighting of Jill Scott. They'd just watched her give a sterling performance playing for Everton in an away game against Manchester City and they were waiting for autographs.

Though Everton had lost, Jill had played brilliantly. She'd become one of Fran's favourite players and it was so exciting to see her play in the flesh. And it was a fraction of the price of an Arsenal season ticket

– any hope of ever seeing Thierry Henry play was out of the question. But at least Fran was getting the opportunity to see her female heroes in action.

Her dad Stephen had taken her to the game. 'I can't believe it,' he said. 'You finally get into a Sunderland player and she flipping defects to Everton.'

'Here she is!' Fran called out excitedly as Jill Scott appeared.

'Oh – hello!' She looked overwhelmed to see the fans waiting for her, clutching pens and shirts.

Fran held up the Number 8 shirt with Scott on the back.

'Thanks for all your support, pet!' said Jill. 'What's your name?'

'Fran's gonna play for England one day,' her dad piped up.

'Dad!'

'Well, fantastic, pet! Who do you play for now?'

'JMA, for the Royals.'

'I hear they've got some really great players coming up.'

Fran beamed.

'Which position do you play?'

'Number Nine. I wanna be a striker first and foremost though!'

'Well, I look forward to seeing you up front on the pitch someday soon! We'll need you if we're gonna ever beat Germany!'

'Nice to hear the accent again,' Jill said to Fran, and joked to Stephen, 'You've definitely lost yours, though!'

It was true. Fran's Geordie twang remained, but for her dad, his had long been replaced by a Reading accent.

Stephen sighed. 'I suppose it had to happen one day.'

*

Deni called up the stairs. 'Fran! Your pasta's ready!'

It was a school night, and Fran was dragging her heels. They were about to go to the Centre of Excellence at Hogwood Park for an analysis meeting. At the end of every season Fran and her mum met with staff at the academy for feedback on player performance. Fran knew she was developing as a player, but she never particularly enjoyed sitting still with her mum, with the coaches opposite, outlining where they felt she could do better.

Her mum said: 'If you don't know what you need to improve on, how can you get better? And even Pelé probably got bad feedback once in a while.'

Fran couldn't help but always fear the worst: that her coaches might suddenly decide she wasn't good enough, and that her dream of playing for England was just that – a dream. She couldn't imagine her life without football now and couldn't shake the feeling that it might be pulled from her.

Her mum gave her a big smile. 'Do you want to stay at Harriet's tonight?'

Fran beamed. 'Oh can I, Mum?'

Harriet was also receiving feedback at the academy. She knew that afterwards her dad would let them both stay up a bit later than usual, as a treat for all their hard work that season, and let them watch the film *Bend It Like Beckham.* They'd seen it so many times but they loved it, especially the Curtis Mayfield song, 'Move On Up'.

'Yeah, make sure you pack your pyjamas!' Fran looked at the treats her mum had prepared and packed for her for later – still in her old lunchbox.

'Aaw, thanks Mum.' She gave her a massive hug.

'Come on, you can do this!' said Deni. 'And if they give you a hard time – they'll have me to contend with!'

Fran met an excited Harriet in the corridor. 'Dad says we can order pizza later! Whatever we want!'

'Extra jalapeño peppers for me!' replied Fran. That was something to look forward to. She just needed to get through this first.

*

Fran and her mum sat opposite Kelly and the managers. As ever, Fran found something else to concentrate on – this time, one of the managers who had a lopsided moustache. It was a distraction, and it meant she wouldn't take anything too seriously as she listened to the analysis.

Kelly gave Fran a big smile before she started talking:

'We feel you've progressed really well this season. You're developing your skills on the wings and becoming a much stronger striker. You're easily one of the fastest in the team and your acceleration over a short distance can cause problems for any defender on the opposing team. You've honed your passing skills and we're really impressed with your finishing too.'

'This all sounds very positive,' said Deni.

'Sounds like there's a "but" coming,' chuckled Fran.

'But,' continued Kelly, on cue, 'I'm particularly impressed with how you've worked on your attitude. Your focus is sharper than ever and you're also much better at managing your emotions if you make any mistakes. Just remember to have a bit more patience when the opportunity opens up to take those strikes – there's no need to hurry it. Take your time and be confident you'll finish.'

'Great!' said Fran. 'When do I join Reading FC then?'

The staff all laughed.

'In good time, Fran,' replied Kelly. 'You're on your way to becoming a scoring machine!'

Fran was delighted. She looked at her mum who was quiet, which was rare for her, and looking off into the distance.

Kelly asked her: 'Are you alright, Mrs Kirby?'

'No, I'm feeling a little queasy, actually. I think... I think I've just got a bit of a headache.'

A few minutes later Fran hurried down the corridor to where Harriet and her dad were sitting.

They could tell something was wrong from her expression.

'Fran? What is it?'

'Mum's not well – she's had to go to hospital.'

Harriet's dad sprung up from his seat. 'We'll go now.'

At the hospital Fran waited for news for what felt like hours with Harriet and her dad.

A doctor approached Fran. 'Could you please call your dad?'

When Stephen arrived they both went down

to the room where Deni was in bed. Before they reached the door, Stephen turned to Fran and said: 'Go to Harriet's, sweetheart. Try and get some sleep. I'll stay with your mum.'

The next morning Fran and Harriet went back to the hospital. At first, Fran was taken aback to see her aunties and uncles from Sunderland there too. For a moment, she was happy to see them all. Then she realised that they were all crying. She felt Harriet grip her hand as her dad turned to her with tears in his eyes. Fran's heart sank as she turned to hug Harriet and began to cry.

CHAPTER 12

KEEP GOING AND CARRY ON

'Okay – see you later!' Fran went to open the car door. Her dad had just dropped her off at football practice.

'Fran, hang on a sec...'

'Yes?'

'What, er, time do you need picking up?'

'The usual, Dad – in about an hour.'

'Shall I just wait here?'

'It's up to you, Dad, I mean, if you've got to be somewhere else...'

'I can wait here... it's a nice evening, I think the footie results are coming on soon anyway.'

'Okay, Dad...'

'Or I could... come and watch?'

'Dad, I'm late – I've got to go!'

'Okay, okay. Just let me know if there's anything you need for football? New kit? Trainers?'

Fran smiled. 'Yeah, don't worry dad, I'll let you know.'

'Great, maybe we could go shopping?'

'Yes, Dad.'

It had been several months since Deni had passed away and Stephen had taken over many of her mother's duties. Fran knew how hard he was trying at his new role – doing his best to be both mum and dad. She felt for him so much as she watched him try to make tea and put snacks together for her games, just as her mum had done.

He'd changed his work shift patterns on the railways so that he could take Fran to her football training, and was taking even more of an avid interest in her playing. Her brother James was also doing his best to support her. He'd been in the middle of his GCSE exams when it had happened, but he'd taken time out to watch more of her matches and offer support.

The whole family did their best to carry on with day-to-day life and in many ways football became a welcome distraction for Fran. There was always something to strive for and focus on in a game – you had a match to win so you couldn't get too lost in your own thoughts. She'd always remembered what the coaches had said to her that night, how happy they were about the changes to her mindset. She was determined to keep going, on and off the pitch – for her teammates, but especially for James and for her dad.

That meant getting up, going to school and just carrying on. Even if the reality was extremely difficult to cope with. Fran still expected her mum to walk through the door every evening just before five as she always had done, ready to take her to practice. Fran realised just how much she missed the little things – singing in the car, the hot cups of cocoa and the kind words. She would have forfeited being 'the best player in the world' as her mum always called her, just to hear her say 'Hello, pet' one more time.

Harriet and her family were incredibly kind and

helped out practically whenever possible, taking Fran to and from training. Although it was rare they ever played on different sides, the girls' different positions on the pitch complemented each other – as a defender, Harriet taught Fran about the different defensive techniques to watch out for, while Fran challenged Harriet with the tricky turns and moves that were becoming her signature.

'Okay, Fran, I admit defeat!' said Harriet. 'There's no getting past your feet today! But I know something I can definitely beat you at!'

On the days when they'd had enough of honing their footballing skills they'd catch the bus down to the nearby Wokingham Superbowl for ten-pin bowling and then squeeze in a game of LaserQuest. It was yet another reason Fran appreciated their friendship so much. Harriet could sense when she needed to switch off and do something completely different.

But these opportunities were rare. Fran regularly stayed late after training with Harriet and other team members, in order to get better. Kelly had told her that she could make her Reading FC debut within the year, and Fran was determined to make that her goal, not least because it gave her something specific to focus on.

'I have a purpose,' she told herself.

Fran had been working her way through the junior teams for years. She couldn't give up now. And she was spurred on by Kelly's goals and ambitions for the team. Since the formation of a women's team in 2006, she had high hopes to take them into premier league women's football.

'We may only be a part-time team at the moment,' said Kelly, 'but I'm going to take you all to the top tier!'

With only four hours a week of training this didn't yet seem achievable for the team. But Kelly had every faith in them, and Fran sensed that it was down to players like her that enabled the team to keep producing quality football every Sunday.

*

Kelly was keen to develop Fran as one of their top players, but she was also aware of the intense pressure that Fran was putting herself under.

'Just take one day at a time, Fran. When you can't do that, just take it one hour at a time.'

No, thought Fran, I have to look ahead to the future. I have to become a bigger and better player.

It wasn't long before Kelly rewarded Fran for her hard work, resulting in Fran's debut at Reading FC, aged sixteen.

CHAPTER 13
RELENTLESS

'Go, Fran, go!' she heard her dad and brother cry in the crowd at the Madejski Stadium, as she made her way out on to the pitch for her first senior game.

As she ran out in her Blues football kit her heart surged with pride as she looked over at Harriet. The night before the game they'd painted their nails blue and white, as had become their customary ritual. They were playing in the southern division against Doncaster Belles, who were one of the toughest sides in the league.

They were both excited to be part of a team that was continuing to excel under Kelly's tutelage.

Before the game, Kelly had told Fran: 'See how

you go in your first season as a winger – then we'll look at changing your position.' She knew that deep down Fran would feel happiest as a striker, but she wanted to see her confidence build, during what she knew was still an incredibly difficult time for Fran. She also wanted to develop her within because she knew offers of American scholarships would be coming her way from various scouts in the USA if they spotted her potential. They'd lost some good players to the prospects they offered – a more established professional league, offering better pay and more opportunities to play and develop with international players out there, a frustrating reality for the team and its manager.

The Belles from Doncaster were renowned for being a strong side with tough players, but from the outset the Blues' formidable defence kept the ball out of the dangerous areas of the pitch. Fran worked incredibly hard in midfield keeping possession from the start. But she was also fearless in helping to create chances up in attack, making as many assists as she did shots on targets. Her pace and technique were relentless up front as she chased after the ball and made perfect crosses to other players. By half-time the Blues were up 2–0 with Fran setting up assists for the team's main striker, Melissa Fletcher.

In the second half they conceded their first goal to the Belles – but it didn't deflate the team. Ten minutes later, Fran spotted an opportunity. She was developing her skill with both feet but still felt more at ease on her left.

In midfield, she picked up a ball and ran down the left flank controlling the ball with her preferred dribbling foot. The defenders proved to be no match for her as she slalomed between them. Outside the penalty box, she assessed her opportunities to pass to other players. There was Melissa who was nearer the penalty box and could easily nudge the ball in. This was the shot the goalkeeper was anticipating as they ran out in her direction.

Without hesitation, Fran took the opportunity to shoot the ball with her left foot, right past the unsuspecting goalie into the right of the net.

GOAL!!!

Fran's debut was hailed as a success by the club and she continued to play well in other matches throughout the season. She was gaining a reputation as a tiny but tough tornado of speed on the pitch, and it wasn't long until she was approached by a scout from Florida in the US, who asked if she'd be interested in playing for the US team Washington Spirit.

Fran was flummoxed. She'd just started her A levels, but the thought of playing football in warmer climes, surrounded by palm trees, was incredibly enticing. Meanwhile, she also received some exciting news from Kelly.

'Fran – guess what? I've been on the phone to the Under-19s England football team – they want you to attend a training camp! Are you free in two weeks?'

'Wow,' thought Fran, 'it's all coming together.'

Her dad, her brother and Harriet were all overjoyed when they heard the news.

'Your mum is watching over you, Fran,' said Harriet, 'her star is shining over you.'

However, there was a nagging feeling at the

back of Fran's mind that she couldn't quite shake off. And a feeling of emptiness, that there was something missing. She always thought that if she just concentrated on fulfilling her dream she'd be okay. She owed it to her mum, who'd been such an incredible support throughout her whole life. But Fran kept returning to the same thoughts. Her mother wasn't there to share it with her. So what was the point of all the hard work without her?

Each day began to feel like a chore. She got up early to train before attending lessons in the sixth form. And then she went to the gym in the afternoon. She'd put together an exercise regime with Harriet that Kelly had recommended, but it wasn't as fun as it had been at the start. Finally, later in the evening, she would return to training.

Fran realised she never had a chance to rest or recharge. And her relentless schedule was beginning to get to her.

One night when she returned home late from another night of training, her dad was waiting up for her.

'Fran, how about a rest, eh? Come with us to Newcastle in a few weeks. It'd be good for you to see the family.'

'I'd love to, Dad, but you know it clashes with the training camp.'

'Ah, okay.'

The day of the training camp arrived. She wished she felt more excited. Or even nervous. Was she exhausted or bored? Or both?

The coach welcomed her enthusiastically, with a look that said: 'We've heard great things about you – now show us what you can do.'

But she couldn't perform any of her usual magic that day at training. Her feet lacked their usual lustre as she ran down the turfs. She was distracted and not as attuned to her team or the opposition. Normally she loved the challenge of getting to grips with new and different players. But today, she didn't really care.

This was a great opportunity and she could feel herself throwing it away. She noticed the coach and the other players looking confused. All of a sudden, she heard a voice inside herself say: 'Stop, it doesn't matter what they think of you. Who are you? Who are you?'

She began to well up a little as she realised she had no idea. She couldn't answer that question anymore. The pressures of football had taken over. She heard the voice again: 'Choose yourself now, Fran.'

She suddenly knew exactly what she had to do. She turned to the coach and said: 'I'm sorry.' Then she went to the changing room and took off her football boots.

She was getting on the train to Newcastle.

CHAPTER 14

TAKING TIME OUT

'Fran!' Her family greeted her with hugs and smiles.

She started to well up as she looked into the familiar faces of people who were close to her mum and who understood the pain she was going through. It was great to see them all again. She looked at her dad, who nodded and smiled.

'I think you're long overdue a break, Fran,' he said. 'All of us are. But you especially, I think.'

Fran put her head on her dad's shoulder and let herself cry in front of him. She'd never done this before but she was done with holding back. She needed the release and as he hugged her tight she knew, at that moment, that nothing mattered except being with her family.

She knew some of her friends and coaches in the footballing world might judge her harshly for quitting the game. The Women's Super League had just been formed, the highest league of women's football in England. There was now the chance for women to play at least semi professionally. So Fran's decision seemed even stranger.

She was missing chances to develop her skills and be challenged. The chance to train with and play for the under 19s England women's team. The chance to play in America. The scout from the US had contacted her to discuss the scholarship offer, but she told them clearly: 'I'm taking some time out.' When people pressed her on how long that period might be, she replied: 'I'm not sure.'

Harriet was still playing as a defender for Reading FC. They'd won their last four games of the season in the Southern Division for the 2009–10 season, and finished as runners-up to Barnet. This meant they'd also secured promotion to the FA Women's Premier League National Division.

Harriet had high hopes for the team moving up the division –Arsenal Ladies and Everton were still the big players. Fran still enjoyed discussing the team's successes with her, although Harriet missed her terribly and didn't think the team were doing as well without her.

'You've left a big void that's for sure, Fran.'

'I just feel worn out, Harriet, it stopped feeling fun to play.'

'We understand, Fran. You've just got so much talent that we don't want to see go to waste.'

'I feel like my whole life has only ever been about football. What about me? It's always been Fran the footballer. But who's Fran without the game?'

'A funny, sweet, kind, hilarious loving person, with or without a football at her feet. But not surprisingly, you've lost the joy of playing. You need this time out. And if and when you decide to return, we'll be here waiting for you.'

'Thanks, Harriet.' Fran felt lost without her mum but Harriet helped to anchor her.

For now, Fran was enjoying the time out away from the pressures of football. She was enjoying fully focusing on her subjects at sixth form college again without the pressures of training, and was considering other careers in physical education that included physiotherapy and coaching. Her mum had always ensured she was able to juggle her schoolwork alongside football, but Fran was relishing the opportunity to give her full attention to it.

And without those pressures of football, a weight started to lift from her shoulders and she started to do things that every other normal sixth-former did. She slept in at the weekends, hung out with friends after A-level classes, and watched films late into the afternoon rather than rushing to training in the evenings. She caught up on books she'd not read and made new friends she'd never really spoken to before in classes.

She continued with some physical activities when she felt the need to let off steam. As well as runs through the Chiltern Hills with Harriet, she joined a gym where she started doing weight training to help develop her core and balance. As she revelled in the simple pleasures of running and feeling the wind in her hair, she began to sense that the smile was returning to her face once again.

She was also enjoying spending more time with her close family.

'What's for dinner, Dad?' she asked as she sailed through the door. 'Oh, don't tell me – macaroni cheese again?'

'Give me a break, Fran – I'm still learning!'

'I know, Dad, I wouldn't want anything else now.'

Meanwhile, her brother James had started a new job at Toys "R" Us and would often come home with the latest toy to hit the market.

'Basically, I'm stuck with two kids!' scoffed Fran.

'It's down to you to make sure we grow up then, Fran,' said her dad.

'More chance of Sunderland winning the division, I think!'

'Oi!'

Occasionally she'd have a fun five-a-side knock around with her brother up on the heath but for the most part, her football boots remained stuffed in a bag at the back of her wardrobe. One Sunday though, a friend at her sixth form college asked her to come and play with his team.

'I dunno...' she replied.

'Oh come on, I could do with some helpful pointers on my game, even if you just come and watch. Or even just to get some coaching practice in? I'll be your test dummy!'

'I suppose I could show you how to do the Cryuff turn!'

'The what?'

'I'll show you!'

Fran watched from the sidelines, but couldn't resist stepping in when they lost their striker at half-time. She was in her element for the next forty-five minutes – running about, shouting orders down the pitch and tying knots in the defence with her moves. They were all exhausted by the end of it, not least the opposition. Fran was the only one with any energy left.

'Flipping 'eck – none of us could keep up with you!'

'Yeah, no surprises you used to play for Reading!'

Fran laughed. She was surprised how much she'd enjoyed it.

At home, as she burst through the door her dad looked up. He was happy to see an extremely big smile on her face.

'Going back next Sunday then, Fran?'

She answered, almost in one breath: 'You know what, Dad – it was really good to play, just for fun. No pressure, no worrying about my performance or letting the team down or wondering where we're going to end up in the division. It was great!'

'I can see!'

CHAPTER 15

WELCOME BACK

Fran continued to play every weekend and began to realise she was looking forward to it each week. Before long she'd joined a Sunday league. Without the pressure of making any mistakes she took more shots on target and was constantly netting goals. Her fighting spirit and desire to score was returning. She felt like a little kid again, running around and having fun.

'You look like you're really enjoying yourself out there, love,' said her dad after coming down to watch her play at one game. 'You're a thorn in the side of those poor defenders, eh?'

'It's good practice, Dad.'

'Practice?' her dad looked at her quizzically.

Fran checked herself. She didn't quite know what she meant by that word, but it had just slipped out. Practice for what? What she'd given up? Was she preparing for something? As she continued to play, compliments from players and spectators flooded in.

'You're just too fast for us.'

'You should be playing professional. Why aren't you playing in one of the Women's Super League's teams?'

She had to admit it. Her love for the game was returning. And as much as she enjoyed playing with the team, she started to long for tougher and stronger opponents again, who would challenge her. The thought of giving more time to professional football didn't seem like such a sacrifice anymore.

She discussed it with Harriet while they played ten-pin bowling one night.

'Only you can make the decision, Fran. We'd all love you to return of course, especially as we've been relegated. Having said that, you seem as though you're back to your old self – maybe you shouldn't rock the boat?'

'Yeah,' agreed Fran. 'I do feel a lot better now. I'm enjoying life again.'

Harriet looked her in the eye, and said:

'You know, she'd be proud of you, whatever you decide. And she'd just want you to be happy too.'

Fran stewed it over for the next few weeks before she dug out the football boots she'd worn for her Reading debut.

'Come on then, time for an airing.'

She remembered buying this pair of cleats with her mum, not long before the night her entire life had changed.

'Okay, Fran,' she said to herself, 'it's time. It's what Mum would have wanted.' She looked in the mirror, smiled and added: 'And it's what *I* want too.'

Kelly looked as though she could jump for joy when she heard the news. She welcomed Fran back with open arms:

'Of course you can come back – we've missed our little Geordie Fran! And, er, no pressure of course... but we could really do with you scoring some goals!'

Reading had been relegated to the FA Women's

Premier League Southern Division for the 2012–13 season.

'This season will be our season with you back!' said Kelly. 'We'll be promoted to Women's Super League!'

Fran thought she might buckle again under this level of pressure, but she was raring to go and couldn't wait to get back on the pitch.

*

Reading were flourishing in the FA Women's Premier League Southern Division and it was, in large part, thanks to Fran's consistent scoring throughout the season.

It was a rainy autumnal day at Barlow's Park, home to Reading FC Women and the team had gotten off to a great start against Queens Park Rangers (QPR).

Fran was dominating the game with her signature tenacity. She rarely lost possession of the ball and was in her element, running up and down both flanks, wrong-footing defenders and cutting in when they least expected it. The opposition were continually disorientated by the pace of her play. They didn't stand a chance.

With a few minutes to go until half-time, Fran got control of the ball and tore down the left flank, dribbling at considerable speed.

She dodged her way between two defenders outside the penalty box, stepping over the ball to confuse them each time. She then tore towards the goalkeeper, without even bothering to look at the defender to her right, who was desperately trying to outrun and tackle her. But she was in too fast. Fran was equally at ease now on both her left and right foot, which left the defenders behind her floundering. In the penalty box, she found a yard of space and kicked the ball with her left foot – her touch was just the right pressure and her technique was perfectly curled as she netted it into the right side of the goal.

GOAL! It was her third of the match!

Fran had scored a hat trick!

They all jumped round cheering at their clear 3–0 lead. Any opportunities for QPR to claw back were now limited. Fran went on to score her fourth goal in the second half, while her tenacity and energy on the pitch lifted the spirits and confidence of the other players. Their winger Becky Jane scored two, then Palmer and midfielder Stacie Donnelly each netted a goal to make the final score 8–0. As they celebrated with Kelly, the team felt as though they were an unstoppable side once again.

At the end of the game, Kelly announced that a new coach was taking over – former Arsenal and Wales midfielder Jayne Ludlow.

'I'm not going far, girls, I'm just moving to be your manager now!'

Fran was sad to hear the news. She'd only just returned and Kelly was such a safe familiar face. She'd known her for so many years now and she'd developed with her so much as a player, she felt like a member of her family.

'She's going to lift this team even more, Fran – just you see.'

Kelly was right. Fran immediately clicked with Jayne who saw Fran's ability from the off, who could easily alternate between that midfield position and a true striker.

'I'm putting you in as a striker, Fran.'

'Yes!' Fran jumped up and down.

CHAPTER 16

PLAYER OF THE SEASON

It was half-time at The Den, home to the Millwall Lionesses. The Royals were feeling the brunt of the Lionesses' experience with staunch long-time players who were all doing a first-rate job of clearing most of the chances Fran and the team created.

The Royals were 2–1 down, but Jayne was confident they could easily equalise in the second half and go on to win. As their top goal scorer, Fran felt the weight of expectation on her shoulders. She also felt the responsibility of rallying the team when they were under pressure.

'Come on! We can do this!' shouted Fran, as they ran back out for the second half.

She knew that if she could just pick up a few more touches from midfield she could make some penetrating attacks and passes on the left wing and attempt some shots on target.

Ten minutes into the second half, Fran saw Stacie pick up a long pass from Harriet Scott. Fran started running down on the left side to get up close to the penalty area. Stacie took it on first touch and instinctively passed it to Fran. Fran wasn't quite in the box but two defenders took her on. She played it safe and passed back to Stacie who was still onside. Stacie went to shoot and it deflected off the goalie. Fran spun around, looking for any opportunity to shoot it back in. Within a split second, she had netted it straight to the back of the net with her left boot.

GOAL!

They'd equalised. Fran felt the energy of the team soar as they leaped around and hugged her. Their prolific goal scorer was not letting them down. Ten minutes later, and buoyed by her earlier goal, she took a shot on target from outside the goal line. She barely looked up as, once again, she netted it low to the right of the goal with her left foot.

GOAL!

Ten minutes later, the whistle blew. The Royals had beaten Millwall Lionesses 3–1. They were now the champions of the FA Premier League Southern Division.

Jayne, Kelly and Fran's family were all present to honour Fran at the Player of the Season ceremony, which was held at the Madejski Stadium. As Fran lifted the trophy and posed for photos with Jayne, Jayne turned to her and said: 'No regrets on returning then?'

Fran beamed from ear to ear.

'None whatsoever.'

*

Fran was still in shock at all she'd achieved that season. She could never have predicted she'd be the top scorer for the season in the FA Women's Premier League Southern Division, scoring thirty-two goals in twenty-one appearances.

In some ways, it was almost as though she'd never

stopped playing football. But she now realised that taking some time out had been the best thing for her to do. It had helped to replenish her energy and remember why she loved the game so much.

'We're so proud of you, Fran,' said her dad.

'Thanks, Dad,' she replied, as tears welled up in her eyes.

Despite her successful return to the team, though, she was still keen to pursue her other passion and interests. She enrolled at Bucks University to study a foundation degree in Applied Coaching Science. She chose it because she wanted to develop her leadership skills and have the opportunity to blend academic study within a professional sports environment.

It was during one of her classes that her phone rang. She picked up.

A voice said: 'I'm calling on behalf of Kay Cossington, head coach for the Under-23 England team.'

Fran's ears pricked up.

'How do you fancy spending the summer in Kazan?' the voice continued.

'Where?'

'It's a beautiful city in Russia and the weather will be incredible, that's for sure. We'd like you to play for Great Britain in the World University Games.'

Fran had heard of the tournament but she was thrilled to hear the words 'play for Great Britain'. She said 'yes' immediately.

Fran soon learnt that she was the only player to be picked from her university. She'd also be playing alongside more experienced players. One of these included Dani Carter who'd helped Arsenal win the inaugural FA WSL title, as well as the 2010–11 FA Women's Cup.

She was a little nervous though too. 'Dad, I've never been that far away on my own!'

He reassured her: 'This will be a great experience for you, pet – your first international tournament!'

CHAPTER 17

KAZAN

Fran first met the rest of the Great Britain team for the 2013 World University Games at the airport. She was joining girls from universities all over the UK – Leeds, Plymouth and Salford. There was also Manchester City's Izzy Christiansen and Demi Stokes.

Among the wide variety of dialects she could hear, Fran soon recognised the familiar accent of Demi Stokes who'd played for Sunderland in the Premier League, and the two struck up conversation almost immediately.

'It's like talking to a member of my family,' Fran laughed.

It was so exciting to have completely new people to play within a team. As much as Fran loved her Reading teammates, especially Harriet, she was looking forward to the fresh challenge and discovering how they would all gel together.

But more than that, she knew her dad was right: meeting and playing against international players would be an invaluable experience, as she'd be joining over 160 countries across the world.

Fran's dream of playing for England looked like it was about to become a reality – she'd already been called up for the Under-23s training camp. But she knew she had to continually improve to make sure it happened.

As the team touched down in Kazan and walked through the airport the hot air hit them. It was July and the city was in the middle of a heatwave. As they stood around the airport, fanning themselves, the nerves suddenly struck Fran. But she also felt excited for all that lay ahead.

In the group stages of the tournament, Fran performed well in the Great Britain matches against

Japan and Brazil. But it was in the quarter-finals match, where they faced Ireland, that she really hit her stride, scoring two of Great Britain's eight goals, in the thirty-seventh and sixty-first minutes. They faced a tough Brazil side at the semi-final, but won 1–0, and went on to meet Mexico in the final.

Mexico had been a strong side throughout the tournament, and had gained a reputation as a scoring machine, just as much as the Great Britain side.

The British team were apprehensive about how this match would play out head on. Their coach Kay Cossington brought them all together before the game, as they heard the cheers for GBR echoing around the Rubin Stadium.

'You just need one or two goals,' said Kay, 'and then that's it – once you've had that breakthrough you're unstoppable, I've seen it with so many of your games. You just need that confidence boost from the initial first goal. Then the floodgates will open. You can win this, girls.'

Fran hung on to each and every one of Kay's

encouraging words. She was still in shock at how much fun she'd had during the tournament scoring goals. Was it allowed to be this fun? Kay was right. Once they got going there was no stopping them. And here she was, playing in her first international final. She enjoyed the atmosphere at Reading games but to draw a crowd from all over the world was unlike anything she'd experienced before. Admittedly, UK fans were thin on the ground but her family had flown out especially for the final. The match was also being televised live on Eurosport. She had to take a moment to digest this. Little Geordie Fran? On the telly? She knew all her family up in Newcastle would be watching.

*

From kick-off, the pace was fast. Mexico took the lead and scored in the first ten minutes. GBR quickly equalised but then the opposition scored again eight minutes later. They weren't leading for long though. Just before half-time, Izzy Christiansen levelled the score to 2–2.

It looked as though neither side would back down.

'Okay, girls, don't let them get ahead,' warned Kay. 'Let's make this ours!'

The second half lost some of the game's earlier momentum. Fran desperately sought to find an opening to score. Finally, her breakthrough came in the eighty-second minute. She saw plenty of room open up in front of her within a confused Mexican defence, as she caught a ball from Izzy in midfield. There was no stopping her once she saw it and she headed forward at speed on her own into the penalty area. She lined up the ball with her right foot and finished low and to the left of the goal, straight past the keeper.

GOAL!!!

The Great Britain team jumped for joy as Fran secured their lead for the first time in the match. Fran sensed the deflation of the Mexican side as the spirits of GBR soared. Within ten minutes they'd scored three more goals – Fran provided an assist for Aileen Whelan, when she passed a curling technical cross from the left.

Fran had to pinch herself as she realised they were

leading by two goals. Only a minute later she picked up a long ball from midfield that the opposition's defenders weren't able to catch. She headed down at speed to wait for it to land in the penalty area. It was a great technical pass brilliantly executed that Fran caught on her right foot. As it bounced and began to roll away, she chased after it, while a defender tried to intercept the ball on her right. But they couldn't reach it before Fran's left boot got there first and slammed it impulsively, yet decisively, into the back of the net.

GOAL!!! She waved her fist in the air and ran back to her teammates to celebrate. They were well ahead, leading more than comfortably. But just to make sure, Danielle Carter-Loblack slammed in yet another goal, their final one, in the ninetieth minute, to make it 6–2.

Afterwards the GBR team talked to the press. 'To play in any international tournament is an honour,' they said. 'But to take away gold?' They were all ecstatic as they clutched their medals close to their hearts.

Their exceptional performance throughout the games was lauded, especially as many had never played internationally before, with accolades flooding in, praising their confidence and creativity.

But it was pint-sized Fran's fresh and raw talent that football pundits were taking notice of, and her reputation as a standout player was cemented when she was acclaimed as 'player of the final'.

As she boarded the plane home, she reflected on her University Games experience. She'd excelled in her first international tournament and proven what she was capable of, not only to a global audience, but also to herself. The games had been a fantastic stepping stone on from club football and confirmation that she was ready to play for England.

CHAPTER 18

KIRBY 9

'YES!'

The girls whooped and cheered as Jayne Ludlow gathered them together at the Madejski Stadium to tell them the news they'd all been hoping for.

'We are now in the FA Women's Super League 2! We've done it, girls!'

All their hard work had paid off and their licence to play in the second-highest division of women's football in England was justly deserved. They'd been granted a licence, along with London Bees, Durham, Aston Villa, Millwall Lionesses, Yeovil Town, Reading, Sunderland, Watford, and Oxford United.

In the 2012–13 season Reading FC Women won

the FA Premier League Southern Division by eight points and a goal difference of forty-one.

'This is an incredible achievement,' said Jayne, 'and a wonderful team effort. But I do think we all need to thank one particularly extraordinary player who got us here.'

Fran was their top scorer for the season in the FA Women's Premier League Southern Division, delivering thirty-two goals in twenty-one appearances.

'Congratulations to our player of the season!' cried Jayne.

Fran blushed as they all turned to her and lifted her up on their shoulders.

'Easy!' she said.

'Another benefit to you being small, eh?' laughed Harriet, who had tears in her eyes. 'You're as light as a feather!'

'Our phenomenal goal scorer!' they all cheered at the top of their voices.

'Guys, stop it!' said Fran. 'It's like Jayne says, it's been a total team effort.'

'We're going to be playing against a higher standard of players now, team,' Jayne prepped them. 'Like Doncaster Belles. But I've every faith you can do it.'

She took Fran aside. 'I want to mix things up a bit and change the formation for this league.' She unravelled a Number 9 shirt.

'I want you as our main striker, Fran. How do you feel about playing in this position?'

Fran's face lit up. 'Yes – I'm ready!'

'Oh I know you are!' Jayne replied. 'I think you're going to go from strength to strength this season. And the club can only benefit from what you've got to give.'

Jayne was right. Fran would continue to help Reading storm through the league in 2014.

*

The Reading side ran out on to the pitch at Rushmoor Stadium in Farnborough. It was a bright sunny day and although they weren't playing at home, the team felt as though the majority of the 4,000 spectators were loyal fans who were enjoying sharing in the joy of The Royals' recent success. Not least her dad and her brother James, who had started taking sweepstakes with his friends on Fran's wins.

She looked down proudly at her blue-and-white kit, now embossed on the back with 'Kirby 9'. She was going from strength to strength in this new position and had a feeling she was going to pull out some magic that day.

She looked over at Harriet who was staring back at her, as if she could read her mind. She gazed across at her fellow strikers who were making an incredible impression on the pitch – the Reading team was continuing to attract great players that included Lauren Bruton from Arsenal and Becky Jane from Chelsea, who'd received a call-up to England.

Fran breathed another sigh of relief that she'd returned to football. She would never want to have missed out on this and was incredibly happy to be sharing this journey with them.

It didn't take long for Fran to make an impact on the pitch, as she quickly made attempts at shooting on target. Within two minutes she was behind the

Durham defence but her shot went wide. However, near misses didn't get to her anymore. She knew her time would come if she kept on attacking. Two more efforts went over the bar, and it was midfielder Lois Roche who made the first breakthrough, scoring after twenty-seven minutes.

Fran vowed to double the lead before half-time. With just two minutes to go before the break, she was down near the penalty area. Two Durham defenders attempted to challenge her when she caught a ball from midfield but she maintained control, pirouetted round and shot towards goal with a brilliant finish.

GOAL!!!

Ten minutes into the second half, Fran netted another after she sidestepped around the Durham defence.

Durham fought back with some valiant efforts, nearly scoring twice, but Fran was just too fast and tenacious. Five minutes later and there was no chance of the opposition making any comeback. Fran wrapped up the game with her third goal.

The crowd were spellbound by her exceptional play, especially her punishing attack against Durham's defenders.

As the crowd left the stadium, they were chatting excitedly about Reading's star player:

'She was in another class today.'

'They can't let her get on the ball – she won't give it away once she's got it!'

The team were celebrating their win, but it was Fran's hat trick that none of the players could stop talking about:

'What a hat trick! I would not wanna be one of their defenders!'

'Outstanding play, Fran!'

'Keep doing that and we're gonna get promoted again!'

But Fran's week was about to get even better. Just a few days later she received a phone call from Mark Sampson, the England women's team manager.

'How many goals have you scored so far this season, Fran?'

'Er...' Her voice wobbled a little as it sunk in who

she was talking to.

'So many, I imagine you've forgotten?'

She laughed. 'It's quite a few.'

'Talented and humble! Well, suffice to say, you're the country's top goal scorer at club – an astonishing twenty-nine goals in twenty-two games! Would you like to take some of that magic to the England team?'

*

Her hands were shaking as she drove over to her dad's to tell him the news personally. She could barely get the car started.

'Dad, I've been called up to the senior England squad. And I'm the first player in Women's Super League 2 they've ever asked!'

His eyes welled up with tears as he hugged her tight. 'Oh, Fran! We're all so proud of you!'

In their inaugural season in the FA WSL, Reading achieved a third place finish in the League, behind promoted Sunderland and runners-up Doncaster Belles. For a second time, Fran finished as top scorer and player of the season with twenty-four goals in sixteen appearances. Her tally included two more hat tricks, against Watford and Doncaster.

After Reading won the division in the 2015 season, they were promoted to the WSL 1. On 10 December 2015 it was announced that Reading would play their home games at Adams Park, the home of Wycombe Wanderers FC, for the next two seasons. All in all, it had been a triumphant few years for Reading – and not least for star goal scorer Fran Kirby.

CHAPTER 19

PLAY WITH A SMILE ON YOUR FACE

Fran was about to board the coach. She was on the way to her debut senior international appearance in an England friendly against Sweden, at Victoria Park, Hartlepool.

Her dad waved her off.

'Can't believe you're off to The Vic!' he said. 'I played for Sunderland there years ago. Give H'angus the monkey a wave for me!'

'Who?'

'He's their mascot!'

'Thanks for that, Dad. As if I wasn't nervous enough already!'

'You're not nervous are you, pet?!'

'Oh no, course not, Dad. I'm only about to make my debut playing for England!'

'Take a dip in the North Sea – that'll sort you out!'

'Yeah – thanks again, Dad!'

On the coach, Fran relaxed a little as she got to know her teammates. Among them was newcomer Jodie Taylor who played as a forward for Washington Spirit in America. Fran knew a lot was riding on Jodie as the fresh new striker, and that she, in the Number 11 position, was also under pressure to do her best on the wing and provide her with great crosses. They both knew that Mark and the rest of the team were pinning high hopes on them. Fran suspected she was a little bit of a wild card, as the only WSL2 player in the team, and she felt had a lot to live up to.

The coach stopped to pick up experienced England duo Casey Stoney and Kelly Smith, and Fran shrank back into her seat as the pair stepped on board. There were whispers for a while that Kelly might be returning to the squad. What a legend, thought Fran, as one of her favourite Number 10-wearing heroes walked past her. She couldn't believe she'd be in the same dressing room as her, let alone potentially on the same pitch.

Fran felt a little intimidated when Kelly came over to say hello but she was so friendly and natural that she immediately felt at ease. Kelly was genuinely interested in her as a player and asked lots of questions about her career so far. Her face broke out into a huge smile when she found it was Fran's first time playing for England. She said: 'Whenever I get nervous I always remember one thing – "play with a smile on your face".'

'Do you still get nervous?' asked Fran.

'Always!' said Kelly, and went on: 'Casey and me, we're not playing this match. We're being "rested".' She winked. 'I think that's Mark's way of saying we're getting on a bit. So we need you younger strikers to get out there and remind us how it's done, yeah? Deal?'

'Deal,' laughed Fran.

'Remember, you're a Lioness now!'

As Fran put her white England shirt on for the first

time, she took a moment to reflect. How surreal that she'd just been chatting to Kelly on the coach, when it seemed like only five minutes ago she'd watched her play on the TV. She remembered her mum's face, telling her in the kitchen that she would play for England for one day. Now she just had to get out there and prove she was up to it.

'Don't doubt yourself, Fran,' she told herself. 'Don't focus on the pressure, just focus on having fun. Like Kelly said – play with a smile on your face.'

Fran's nerves soon dissipated as she walked out onto the field and heard the supportive cheers of the England crowd. She was on the attack as early as possible. In the first minute one of the Swedish opposition, Nilla Fischer, lost the ball in the penalty area. Fran saw a chance and took a shot on target. It soared over the top of the net and she leapt up in frustration. But she knew there would be more opportunities.

It wasn't long until another chance came, when Steph Houghton shot a long pass down the midfield.

'Go on England! Go on England!' the crowd

roared as Fran played a pass to Jodie. It was blocked but Fran continued to make confident attacks at defenders. Experienced midfielder Karen Carney broke through just before half-time to make the score 1–0. But Fran's efforts paid off in the fifty-third minute. She picked up a brilliant ball from Eni Aluko in the penalty area, and then sped into the box with a defender chasing her down. In a flash, and almost without looking up, she curled a perfect ball inside the far post with her right foot.

Fran was in shock as she saw the ball hit the back of the net. Had she really just scored her first goal in her international debut?

When she felt Eni Aluko and Lianne Sanderson thump her on the back and the rest of the team leap around her she knew it was real. The euphoria had sunk in. She was only twenty-one and she'd just scored for England. She was officially one of the team now, and they all crowded around to congratulate their talented new striker.

Shortly afterwards, Fran – along with Jodie Taylor – was named in England's twenty-three-player squad for their World Cup qualifier against Wales on 21 August 2014 at Cardiff City Stadium.

There were no guarantees yet, but Fran was well on her way to playing in the 2015 World Cup.

CHAPTER 20

THE PROFESSIONAL

Change was in the air at Reading FC. At the end of their highly successful 2013–14 season, Jayne Ludlow moved on to become Manager for Wales women's national team.

'Thanks so much for all you've done for me,' Fran told Jayne. 'You've really believed in me and helped me to become a much more creative player. I've felt a real freedom on the pitch, thanks to you.'

'And in return you've given a lot back to the team,' Jayne replied. The club was now tipped for promotion in 2015.

'You've always had the talent within you,' Jayne went on. 'And I think we're only just starting to see the best of you. There's much more to come.'

Jayne's prediction would be correct, and Fran would continue to flourish as a familiar face, Kelly Chambers, returned to coach and manage the team. Fran's skills delighted audiences at the 2014 Continental Cup that summer. Reading faced the cup holders Arsenal in a group stage match at Rushmoor Stadium in Farnborough.

Before the game, Kelly said: 'Everyone's predicting an easy home win for the premier team. And we're up against England veterans like Casey Stoney and Alex Scott. But I know what you're all capable of.'

Fran and the team grinned.

'Let's show them what we're made of.'

Throughout the match Reading's performance against Arsenal was strong, barely offering their opponents the opportunity to break through its defence – their only option was to shoot from long range.

But it would be Fran, wearing the Number 11 shirt, who would shine yet again.

In the opening minutes of the game she picked up

a long pass from midfield as she waited in the wings. The crowd gasped as she caught the ball on first touch and flicked it over the head of the Japanese international Yukari Kinga near the halfway line. No defender could get near her as she sped into the penalty box. From there the space was clear as she dribbled a bit further then calmly finished, putting it past the keeper with her right foot – right into the left of the net.

GOAL!!! The crowd roared their appreciation as her teammates fell about her laughing and hugging.

But there was more to come. In the second half she picked up a pass from Becky near the penalty box. She was nearly brought down by a defender but she didn't give up, twisting and turning her way back into a position to attack. She regained control to provide an assist for Lauren Bruton to double the lead. They won the match 2–0.

Kelly gave her a huge hug after the match.

'Go Fran! You've surpassed yourself!' Fran and the team's performance had defied all expectations of what a tier two club was capable of.

*

Stephen and James were beaming with pride.

'Front page of the *Tilehurst News!*' said Stephen. 'My little girl!'

Fran laughed. 'Yes, I've made it to the Tilehurst tabloids!'

'Don't you scoff! This is an incredible achievement. You'll be in the broadsheets in no time.'

He read aloud: '"At just twenty-one years of age the striker is one of the most promising prospects in the country – and will now become Reading FC's first ever full-time player ahead of the 2015 WSL 2 campaign".' In other words, Fran had been awarded a professional contract.

'Thanks, Dad. It means I'll be able to train every day.'

'You'll actually be training with the boys?'

'You got it – I'll be alongside the Reading team every day. It means I've even more time to get better and better.'

'It's brilliant news.'

Fran had been on the brink of tears when Kelly first told her the news.

'You've supported me ever since I was a kid... now this?'

'You completely deserve it,' said Kelly. 'With you at the helm we'll get promoted next season no problem.'

They both knew that if the club was promoted it would also give more women the chance to turn professional.

'Thank you, Kelly,' said Fran. 'It's important to me that I inspire other players too.'

'You do, you're an inspiration.'

To top off her successful season Fran achieved WSL 2 Player of the Season, along with WSL 2 Top Scorer. In addition, she was also nominated for the Women's Super League 2 Players' Player of the Year Award.

*

It was a gorgeous spring day in April 2015. As Fran walked out, at the Academy Stadium in Manchester for England's game against China PR, she felt excited but nervous.

It was a 'friendly' pre-match but Fran knew that her inclusion in the World Cup England squad that summer, just a few months later, depended on her performance. It wasn't her first time putting on the Number 10 shirt – she'd already played against the US in Milton Keynes earlier that year in February – but she knew it always came with a certain amount of pressure when playing for your country.

Fran thought of the greats who had worn it before her, such as Kelly Smith who had texted her a 'good luck' message that morning. The England veteran was about to retire and had already namechecked Fran as one of her favourite players to 'watch out for'. Fran hoped with all her heart she could live up to the expectations as the record goal scorer passed the baton onto her. Fran turned to Jodie Taylor, who she knew was feeling just as nervous. She nodded back at her as if to say: 'It's okay – we've got this.'

It took just fifty-nine seconds for England to make a breakthrough. Fran picked up a long ball from Siobhan Chamberlain, the goalkeeper. She ran at pace and delivered a technical pass to Jodie in the penalty box, who slotted in the team's first goal at close range. Straight after she scored, she ran over to Fran to give her a huge hug.

'What a belter you passed me, Fran – thank you!'

With the first goal behind them, there was no stopping the duo. They were away. Ten minutes later it was Jodie's turn to assist, when she passed to midfielder Jordan Nobbs near the penalty box. She shot a powerful cross into the penalty area, which Fran picked up to belt past the goalie with her right foot.

GOAL!!!

Jordan, Jodie and Fran all leapt round celebrating their 2–0 lead, and so early in the game. The match ended with a 2–1 victory for England and the team left in high spirits.

Fran didn't want to get her hopes up too high about her World Cup place until she had final confirmation. She booked a holiday with Harriet to take her mind off it.

She was lying on a beach soaking up the sun when her phone rang. It was a UK number.

Harriet looked over expectantly as Fran took the call.

'Hello Fran. How's your holiday?'

Fran recognised the voice straight away. It was Mark Sampson, the England manager. Her heart skipped a beat and her hands started to shake. She could barely find the words to respond as he continued:

'Get as much rest as you can, you're going to need it if you decide to come to Canada.'

'Canada? What?'

'You're in the squad if you want it, Fran.'

He rattled off more details as she screamed in delight, and Harriet ran over to celebrate.

'I've put you in at Number 22. I hope you don't mind you're not Number 10 this time. I've put Karen in as a more experienced player.'

'Yes, yes, of course!' shrieked Fran. 'I'm just amazed... oh thank you, Mark!'

'Well you've been playing so brilliantly, of course I was going to put you in.'

'Thank you – it's just, it's still so surreal to hear!'

He chuckled. 'Can't wait to see you play, Fran.'

'Mark, thanks for taking this chance on me. I know I'm a bit of a wild card, but you won't regret it, I promise.'

'What? You're a top pick, Fran.'

'But a lot of teams still don't know me. Thanks to you and the team for putting your trust in me.'

He laughed. 'Yes, it means the opposition will underestimate you. Let them do that at their peril.'

She hung up and looked at Harriet in disbelief.

'Two years ago,' she said, 'I wouldn't have thought I'd be anywhere near this. I can't believe I've been picked.'

'Little Geordie Fran's come a long way, eh?'

CHAPTER 21

MINI MESSI

Fran had been in Canada with the team for one week and they were all revelling in the welcome they'd received from the Canadians in the city of Moncton. On arrival, the girls had all been offered free upgrades on their hired cars.

'What's the catch?' asked Jodie.

'No catch! Welcome to Canada, ladies! And good luck!'

As Fran walked out at Moncton Stadium, facing a crowd of 13,000, she thought how happy and lucky she was to be playing for England and travelling to incredible host countries. But the whole team was feeling the pressure that day.

It was only England's second match of the

tournament but they'd lost their previous match against France a week earlier, conceding one goal. Fran hadn't come on until the sixty-eighth minute.

Now they faced Mexico. This was Fran's first starter match and she wanted to make an impact. They all knew it was crucial that England scored in the match. Otherwise, they were going home. It didn't matter who netted the goal. But deep down, Fran wanted to justify Mark's decision for taking a chance on her.

Before the match Mark had gathered them all together and said: 'Whatever happens, before you hang up your England shirts today, I want you to think about who got you to this point.'

But Fran was already thinking of her inspiration. She was thinking about her as the team lined up and prepared to sing the national anthem.

'Let today be the day, Mum', said Fran to herself. 'Let me do this for you.'

Singing the anthem with the rest of the team was still a relatively new experience for Fran. But each time she found it produced a peculiar mix of emotions for the team – the adrenalin was coursing through their veins, yet it was also a private time of reflection for each player, as they contemplated the special people in their lives to whom they were dedicating their performance.

The whistle blew for kick-off. From the start both sides took plenty of chances and each team's goalkeeper made great saves. But no-one could break through and the game remained scoreless throughout the first half. By half-time, the England side were frustrated, especially as they knew they'd been playing well.

Mark told them: 'You've dominated most of this game, girls and rarely been out of possession of the ball. Don't give up, girls. Keep calm. The breakthrough will come.'

Fran had hoped that breakthrough would come in good time too. But she felt the team's energy flag a little in the second half.

'Come on, Fran, keep pushing through. Keep going,' she said to herself as she kept up her pace and momentum, always looking for chances near the penalty box. As the sun beat down on the stadium, it was beginning to feel like a long game. They were heading towards the last twenty minutes. As the game remained goalless they desperately needed a shift in their performance.

Then Fran spotted a challenge from the opposition in midfield. Karen Carney had sidestepped some persistent defenders and gained control of the ball. Fran immediately ran at speed towards the penalty area when she saw Karen pass to an attacker who was further up ahead than her. It deflected off a defender. Fran caught it. She ran with it into the box. She felt Mexican player Verónica Pérez running up on her left side, desperate to kick it away. Fran knew she had to act soon. With a drop of the shoulder, she got through two defenders and poked the ball to the left of the goal. Her heart sank as it hit the post – no! But then relief washed over her as it rolled into the net.

GOAL!!!

Fran waved her arms in the air ecstatically, as she ran towards the substitutes on the bench to celebrate, with a gigantic smile on her face. She'd scored England's first World Cup goal – giving them the lead they so desperately needed – and proved to Mark and the world what she was capable of.

Fran's goal raised the whole team's spirits. Within ten minutes, Karen doubled the lead with a header to make it 2–0. Even though they then conceded a late goal in extra time, England had their first win behind them.

Excited journalists gathered to hear Mark Sampson speak in front of the cameras.

'I am delighted. And yes, relieved. We took some flak after the France game, but the players responded well.'

Then he added, with a smile: 'Special players step up at special moments. Fran Kirby is our mini Messi.'

Fran was also lauded for 'showing the composure England had been lacking in front of goal'.

As Fran walked back into the dorm that night, the girls all started chanting: 'Mini Messi! Mini Messi!'

Fran blushed and started laughing. 'Stop it! We've got a way to go yet!'

Later, Jodie took her aside and said: 'Your mum was looking out for you today. She nudged that ball in from the post.'

Fran smiled. That night she would go on Twitter and dedicate the goal to her mum.

Her father and brother, who had been watching from the stands, also celebrated with the team later.

'Thanks, little sis!' James said to her, by way of congratulation. 'Me and my mates all had bets on you'd score at least once – in the second half too! You're making me money!'

Fran turned to her dad. 'Go on, Dad, where's the feedback, there must be some?' As Fran's career had progressed, her dad had delighted in giving her more pointers on how to improve her game.

'No, Fran – I'm over the moon.'

'Come on, there must be something...'

'Well, okay. In the first half you were quite quiet... but in the second half – you were a lot better!'

'Thanks, Dad – I knew I could rely on you!'

Fran genuinely appreciated that he'd always tell her what he really thought and give her honest feedback – even when she had just scored the first England goal in the World Cup!

Later on in the tournament, Fran was out of the team, due to injury. But she was still there to cheer England on as they beat Canada in the quarter-finals to a crowd of 54,000 in Vancouver. She also watched from the sidelines and celebrated with the rest of the team as they won the third place play-off against Germany. The England team's reputation, as a strong side to contend with, was cemented, as they took the bronze medal.

On their return to the UK, the team were delighted to hear that British audiences had been following England's success. Up to 2.5 million people watched each game, with 11.9 million watching them take third place. This was even despite the kick-off times, which due to the time differences, were later in the UK.

The England team – in fact, all of women's global football teams – could feel the tide of support was rising for the female game. Not least when it was producing new and exciting players that were garnering comparisons to world-class players.

CHAPTER 22

NEW CLUB

After Fran's performance at the World Cup – plus another successful season with Reading that led to their promotion to WSL 1 – the premier clubs soon came knocking. They were competing to sign up the talents of England's little Messi, and Fran was soon in negotiations with Reading regarding transfers.

'Who wants a piece of you today, Fran?' asked her dad.

'Well, it's looking like it's between Arsenal and Chelsea at the minute!'

'Who would have thought... you loved Thierry Henry so much. And now you might be playing for his team.'

'I know. It was always my dream to play for Arsenal. But I've given it a lot of thought. I think I'm going to go with Chelsea.'

'Because they're top of the league?'

'It's not just that. I think the whole team has got a winning mentality.'

But it was her meeting with Chelsea's manager Emma Hayes that clinched it. Fran instantly warmed to her broad smile and direct way of talking.

'We've had our eye on you for a while, Fran. I think you're the missing piece for our team.'

Fran was particularly looking forward to seeing how well she'd fit with the other players up front. She knew Eni Aluko from the England team, but she was also looking forward to playing alongside the talented South Korean midfielder Ji So-yun and the winger Gemma Davison.

But just as Fran was about to sign the contract, Manchester City approached her. They were willing to pay even more than the sizeable amount Chelsea had already offered.

'Let the bidding wars commence!' her dad

laughed. 'My little girl – in so much demand.'

James beamed with pride. 'I'm going to start taking bets on which other teams will wade in!'

But Fran's mind was made up. 'No, I'm definitely going with Chelsea. Manchester is too far away.'

'You sure, pet?' her dad responded.

Fran looked at her brother and dad. 'Yes. I think I'd miss the pair of you winding me up half the time. What with your footie feedback and all, Dad.'

They both laughed but Fran could tell they were relieved at her decision.

Leaving Reading behind for London would be hard, though. She thought of all the nights on her way to training at Hogwood Park with her mum. It was as though she was properly leaving her childhood behind.

Kelly tried not to cry as she hugged Fran goodbye. 'I'm happy for you, really I am. We know you've got to go on and grow and keep developing.'

'Grow? No I think I'm stuck at this height for good now, Kelly!'

'Little Geordie Fran!'

They laughed.

'I couldn't have done it without you, Kelly. Really, both you and Jayne have made me the player I am today.'

For Fran, the last few months had been a whirlwind of change and new opportunities for her. But she remained positive about her decision and knew she was taking the right step forward in her career.

*

After Fran pulled on her Number 14 shirt, she looked down at her bright pink nails in the dressing room. She'd painted them the night before with her teammates, who were now new recruits to one of her oldest and most favourite pre-match rituals. This time she'd let Eni choose the colour.

She checked the fit of her boots one last time. Yes, they felt great. She'd worn them in throughout training, which was always her preference before a big game. Most footballers she knew had a couple of 'superstitions' they followed before a match but they'd certainly served her well throughout her career. And she hoped they'd help her deliver some magic in her next match.

She was about to walk out at the Wheatsheaf Stadium with her Chelsea teammates. They faced Sunderland Ladies. She chuckled to herself. Why did it have to be Sunderland? Her poor dad. She knew he'd be genuinely torn as he cheered her on against his home side. But she knew he'd also be incredibly proud if they won. If the match ended in victory they'd become Women's Super League 1 Champions for the first time.

'Ready, Fran?' Eni and Gemma interrupted her thoughts.

'I am!' cried Fran as she high-fived them both. 'But are Sunderland ready?!'

'No-one's ever ready for mini Messi!'

'Don't mess with mini Messi!'

They all laughed. Fran realised the nickname gave her quite a lot to live up to and she'd felt the pressure of it ever since Mark had first tagged her with it back in the summer.

'Everyone expects me to be shooting fifty goals

a minute!' she said to her dad. But she felt more relaxed about the accolades now. The summer already felt like a long time ago and she was getting into her stride with Chelsea, and proving that she was no one-hit wonder.

She'd joked that the transition into 'the Blues' wasn't that much of a change as her new kit was 'practically the same colour' as the one she'd worn in The Royals back in Reading. But it hadn't taken long to fit in and within weeks her new team felt like one big family.

Just before the whistle blew for the game against Sunderland, Eni turned to Fran with an excited expression on her face and said: 'You'll never guess who's in the crowd. John Terry!'

Fran's face broke out into a huge infectious smile, a feature of hers that was becoming as well-known and loved as her quick-paced feet. She whooped. 'Then let's show him what we can do!'

Right from the kick-off, Chelsea controlled the pace of the game. Within seven minutes Eni burst down the left flank and shot a long pass towards goal that Ji netted to open the scoring. There were cheers around the stadium as the girls hugged each other tight, happy to have secured the lead so early. From the first time Fran had played with Chelsea she'd felt a particularly strong bond with the team's winger Gemma – they seemed to have an innate feel for where each other was on the pitch. Just before half time they proved what a dynamic pair they made as Gemma shot a cross into the penalty area for Fran to finish. They leapt around together in delight.

And neither of them was done yet. Later in the match they demonstrated the strength of their partnership once again when Fran ran onto a perfect pass from Gemma, before finishing coolly. Another huge smile broke out across her face as she skidded on the pitch and fell to the ground to celebrate with her teammates. They'd conceded no goals. The championship was well within their reach.

'Brilliant goal, Fran!'

'I'm so happy with that one!' she cried.

Eni scored once more to make it 4–0. When the whistle blew for the end of the match, both John

Terry and manager and coach Emma Hayes ran on to the pitch to celebrate with them.

Emma grabbed Fran and hugged her. 'I knew you were our missing piece!'

'Well, I really feel like I belong here!' replied Fran as tears of happiness ran down her face. In her first season she'd helped Chelsea secure their first FA WSL title: a league and cup double.

CHAPTER 23

RAY OF HOPE

Fran watched in disbelief from the sidelines. It was April 2018 and there was a beautiful clear blue sky at the Wheatsheaf Stadium that day. Fran thought The Blues would be celebrating an easy victory over Manchester City in the sun later that day (despite the fact her childhood hero Jill Scott was playing for the opposition). But it wasn't turning out as they'd expected. It was the Women's FA Cup semi-final and City had just taken the lead after half-time, while Chelsea were yet to score. It looked as though the away team were destined for their first ever final.

How was this happening? Fran felt frustrated. She was sitting on the sidelines as a substitute, but wanted to get out on the pitch and make a difference. They were already well into the second half, and Chelsea desperately needed a ray of hope.

Finally, in the seventy-sixth minute, Emma turned to Fran. 'Okay, you're on.'

Fran rushed onto the field, determined to equalise for her team. But she couldn't find any spaces in defence or make as many penetrating runs as she normally did. She looked over towards Gemma who seemed equally frustrated. She'd made some great shots on target throughout the match but seemed a little lost without Fran. But then their breakthrough came.

With only a few minutes of regulation time to go, Ji scored from a curling free kick. Fran sighed with relief. They'd scraped through into extra time by the skin of their teeth. Ji's goal had lifted their spirits though. Chelsea started to get better possession of the ball and kept striving to make assists and shots on target – all were denied, though.

But it was Fran Kirby who scored in the 123rd minute, just in the nick of time – and Chelsea were on their way to Wembley for the final. Although they would lose there to Arsenal a month later, Fran's reputation remained intact, as a prolific goal scorer who was also a last-minute game threat.

*

'Aaagh!' Fran cried out as a sharp pain shot through her knee and she fell to the ground.

She'd just collided with a Liverpool Ladies defender at Chelsea's home ground in a 50-50 challenge. They were only fifteen minutes into the game and the pressure was on. Liverpool's Katie Zelem had scored in the first minute. It hadn't taken long for Chelsea to equalise – Karen Carney had scored eight minutes later – but Fran knew the team couldn't afford for her to be out of the game, regardless of the pain she was in.

As she lay there she remembered falling to the ground all those years ago when playing against the Renegades. It made her feel better, despite the pain she was in. When she'd fallen in the mud at the Madejski Stadium, with the boys jeering around her, she never would have predicted she'd end up here.

What had her teammates said to her then? 'You've got to get back up, you've got to play on.' She must do the same now.

'Okay,' Fran told herself, 'you're fine. No worries.'

She winced as she got up and limped down the pitch. Gemma looked across at her, concerned. Fran gave her the thumbs up, and then glanced down at her knee again. It was swollen but she would be okay.

All of ten minutes later she scored to put Chelsea in the lead. Her teammates ran over to celebrate with her. By half-time they were 4–1 up.

'You've got this, girls!' said Emma in the changing room as the delighted team evaluated their play. Fran was happy they were all playing well and getting the goals in. She did her best to focus on that rather than the pain in her knee, which was getting worse.

'I'm fine, I'm fine!' she reassured Eni, Gemma and Ji, but they could tell something wasn't quite right as they looked down at her swollen knee.

'You might want to get that looked at, Fran. We can play on.'

'It's just a bit of bruising,' said Fran.

In the sixty-third minute, Fran scored her second goal. Her fellow strikers ran over to celebrate.

'Wow!' they all cried. 'You can even score goals with a bad knee! You're amazing, Fran!'

She grinned through the pain. She'd netted four times in the last three matches. She wasn't about to slow down now. Chelsea went on to win 6–3. As the team celebrated Fran continued to ignore the pain in her knee. She was determined to carry on playing that season.

CHAPTER 24

RECOVERY

'Yum – they smell delicious!' Fran called out.

Gemma was cooking up burritos in the flat they shared together, located close to the Chelsea training ground at Cobham. Fran enjoyed being close to her work, but it also meant she could drive to her family and Harriet back in Reading easily.

'Ow!' Fran cried out in pain as she attempted to get up off the sofa and walk across to the kitchen.

'Okay,' said Gemma, with a stern look on her face. 'Enough is enough, Fran. You can barely walk! You've got to go and get that knee properly looked at.'

Fran finally relented. She was still playing in games

and scoring goals, but she knew she couldn't carry on like this.

In the medical room at Chelsea, Fran waited for the scan results. The physio looked at her gravely.

'You should not have continued playing on it, Fran. Even you aren't a superhero.'

Fran's heart sank and she suddenly suspected the worst. Visions of her watching her England teammates play Euro 2017, while she was stuck on a sofa, fell into her mind.

'Oh no! How bad is it?'

'Your knee's fractured but the good news is you won't need surgery. Just plenty of rest and rehab. You are very lucky. Don't ever take this risk again. If something hurts that bad, there's something wrong.'

Fran felt the urge to giggle. 'I've been playing with a fractured knee?'

'Hmm,' the consultant replied. 'Maybe you are a superhero.'

Fran heaved a sigh of relief. She had been lucky that time.

She felt upbeat for the first few weeks. She knew

she'd soon bounce back from this and be ready for training for the Euros. She went to Cobham every day for rehab and thanked her lucky stars she had access to their state-of-the-art facilities and the best team physios. For the first few weeks it felt quite fun and relaxing. She got to know the male Chelsea team better too, and became friends with players César Azpilicueta and David Luiz. She made light of her injury whenever she could, as she knew staying upbeat and seeing the funny side would help her heal.

'I feel like I'm on a spa break!' she called out to César and David as they walked past her in the hydrotherapy pool. 'I'm booked into ultrasound treatment and magnetic therapy next!' But as her weeks of convalescence turned into months, she became frustrated that her knee wasn't healing faster.

For all her hard work with the physios, she had suffered setbacks. There was deep internal bruising, which would take a long time to get better. She wasn't able to train in the gym either, which she really missed. More than anything she hated not playing. As supportive as her teammates were, she felt frustrated sitting on the sidelines watching them train.

She turned to Gemma in despair. 'When will it heal?'

Gemma gave her a hug. 'Not knowing must be really difficult. Let's get a dog. I think you need another friend around.'

As soon as Fran set eyes on the little cockapoodle that Gemma brought home she was smitten.

'Aaw! He's adorable!'

She looked into his big brown eyes and ruffled his black and brown fur. 'I'm calling him Cody!'

Fran took her little companion with her everywhere – to rehab, training and back to her family in Reading. She found that looking after him and taking him for walks every day lifted her spirits.

'Great idea, Gemma, thanks. He's really given me something else to focus on.'

*

Almost a year later, after her injury, England manager Mark Sampson named her as part of his squad for the

Euro 2017 championships. She was only just back in training but this announcement spurred her on to do well in the spring series.

'Thank you, Mark! Thank you for believing in me again!'

'Always!' he replied.

'I'll prove to you I'm worth it.'

'I know you will. But please go easy on yourself. Make sure you're 100 per cent before this tournament. There's no point risking another muscle injury.'

'I know, Mark – thank you!'

CHAPTER 25

YOU BETTER START EARLY

Fran sat on the sidelines watching her team play an away match at Eppleton Colliery Welfare Ground, home to Sunderland Ladies. It had felt great to pull her Number 14 shirt back on again that afternoon.

It was the first half and Chelsea were doing brilliantly. She'd already watched newcomers Erin Cuthbert and Ramona Bachmann score, as well as old pals Karen and Ji. By half-time Chelsea were 5–0 ahead.

Fran was over the moon for them all but was itching to get on the pitch and join in the fun by the second half. She turned to the physio and with a big smile said: 'I don't care how I play, all I want to do is get on the pitch and run around a little bit.'

Towards the last twenty minutes of the match she got her chance as Emma substituted her for Ramona. Nothing could have prepared her for the response she received, as she leapt up and tore towards the pitch. Cheers reverberated around the stadium and fans stamped their feet shouting: 'We love you Fran!' and 'Go Fran!'

She struggled to hold back the tears as she reached her teammates. Then she heard the crowd start chanting:

You better start early
To keep up with Kirby
A jinking run, a perfect pass
She's a player of pure class!

Fran looked round in confusion.

'What's that about?!'

'It's the new Euro song!' said Karen.

Fran started laughing. 'Unbelievable! Women's football has its own songs now?'

'Thanks to players like you!' said Ji.

Did she still have the magic, though? Fran asked herself, as the game continued. She had been away a whole year, after all. But all doubt soon left her as she concentrated on the joy of playing.

'How have I missed this!' she cried out as she ran up and down the pitch getting on the attack. Within only two minutes she nearly scored on an assist from Karen, but her shot whizzed just past the post.

'It's coming,' she thought to herself, 'just keep going.'

In the eightieth minute she ran down into the penalty box on the left flank to pick up a long pass from Karen. She caught it on first touch, let it bounce and then darted around the goalkeeper before slotting it into the left of the goal. There was absolute pandemonium in the stadium as everyone celebrated the return of Chelsea's goal-scoring hero.

'Guys, I can't breathe!' gasped Fran as all her teammates ran over to rugby tackle her to the floor and hugged her tight.

'You're back Fran – you're back!'

Even Emma ran on to the pitch to celebrate.

'Careful of her knee, guys!' she warned them all.

Just five minutes later Fran slammed another shot into the net with her right foot. Chelsea went on to win 7–0. The team were on an absolute high to have won – but more than that, they were just happy to have Fran back to her fit and fighting self.

*

As Fran lined up with the England team she looked up into the crowd at the Rat Verlegh Stadium in the Dutch city of Breda. Somewhere in the crowd of spectators sat her dad and brother, both so proud to see her play in her second international and help England get this far in the Euro 2017 tournament. If they won this match they'd go through to the quarter-finals.

Fran put her hand on her heart as she sang the national anthem. She thought of her mum's bright smile and kind words. She knew that she would be bursting with pride, had she been there with them in the stadium.

'Come on, Mum,' as she always said, 'help me get one in today.'

The whistle blew for the start of the match. Fran's request to her mum was answered sooner than either she or her side could have expected. With barely sixty seconds on the clock, Fran put England in the lead.

'I don't believe it!' she shrieked.

Neither could her teammates: 'That was incredible, Fran!'

England conceded no goals, and in the eighty-fifth minute Jodie Taylor slotted in a second goal to secure their victory. They were through to the quarter-finals. England went on to beat France in their next game but lost out to Netherlands in the semi-finals. However, it was clear that they were now a strong and formidable side to contend with.

After the tournament, the players paid tribute to Mark's predecessor Hope Powell for the work she'd put into achieving this.

*

'It's not been a bad season for you, has it Fran?'

It was early 2018 and Fran had just picked up a trophy for Ladies Players' Player of the Year. The presenter read out the other accolades she'd already received that year – PFA Womens' Players' Player of the Year and Chelsea Players' Player of the Year.

'Yeah,' said Fran with a smile, 'it's not been bad. The individual awards are great, but it always comes down to how you impact your team.'

Fran loved to be an integral part of a winning side. In April she'd been instrumental in helping Chelsea win the FA Cup in front of 45,423 fans at Wembley. Just four days later she'd helped the team reach the top of Women's Super League One.

But already, she was looking ahead to the World Cup in 2019 and working with the new England manager Phil Neville. The days of being 'little Geordie Fran' or even 'Mini Messi' were long behind her. Now, she was Fran Kirby with the potential to become the best player in the world.

Reading

- FA Premier League Southern Division: 2012–13

Portland Thorns FC

- FA Women's Super League: 2015, 2017–18
- FA WSL Spring Series: 2014–15, 2017–18
- Women's FA Cup

International

- FIFA Women's World Cup: Third Place

Individual

- WSL 2 Player of the Season: 2013
- WSL 2 Top Scorer: 2014
- PFA Player's Player of the Year: 2018
- Football Writers' Women's Footballer of the Year: 2018
- Chelsea Players' Player of the Year: 2018

KIRBY

14 & 10

THE FACTS

NAME: Frances Kirby

DATE OF BIRTH: 29 June 1993

AGE: 25

PLACE OF BIRTH: Reading, Berkshire

NATIONALITY: British

BEST FRIEND: Harriet

Current Club: Chelsea

POSITION: Forward

THE STATS

Height (cm):	**157**
Club appearances:	**83**
Club goals:	**92**
Club trophies:	**4**
International appearances:	**40**
International goals:	**13**
International trophies:	**0**
Ballon D'ors:	**0**

★★★ **HERO RATING: 88** ★★★

GREATEST MOMENTS

Type and search the web links to see the magic for yourself!

1 3RD AUGUST 2014
ENGLAND 4–0 SWEDEN

https://www.youtube.com/watch?v=gTxGmwHSrP4

After a few near misses, Fran breaks through and scores in the fifty-third minute in her debut senior appearance for England. Their manager Mark Sampson describes her as an 'exciting and creative player'.

2 13TH JUNE 2015
MEXICO 2–1 MONCTON

https://www.youtube.com/watch?v=lXb21MQSTb4&t=27s

Fran takes the pressure off England when she scores the crucial goal that keeps them in the tournament. At the time, Fran is still playing for Reading FC Women. England go on to win the bronze medal.

3 17TH APRIL 2016
CHELSEA 2–1 MANCHESTER CITY

https://www.youtube.com/watch?v=sc7iKqTnWB4

When Manchester City take the lead after half-time, it looks as though Chelsea are close to losing. With only a few minutes of regulation time to go, they equalise. Fran goes on to score the winning goal in extra time, so that Chelsea FC Women can return to Wembley Stadium.

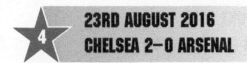

4 23RD AUGUST 2016 CHELSEA 2–0 ARSENAL

https://www.youtube.com/watch?v=67UNI5An_kE

Arsenal are renowned as one of the toughest teams in the WSL but, in 2016, Fran proved with two goals that determination and a never-give-up attitude is crucial. For goal number one, her first touch takes the ball beautifully over the keeper and she scrambles after it on hands and knees to make sure it goes over the line! Her second goal shows excellent positioning: 'right place, right time!'

PLAY LIKE YOUR HEROES

THE FRAN KIRBY 'SPRINT AND DINK'

SEE IT HERE YouTube

https://www.youtube.com/watch?v=2l0eElIAhBY

STEP 1: Get practising your lung-busting sprints – you'll need to be fast for this to work!

STEP 2: Time to put all your running practice to good use. Wait for a teammate in midfield to get the ball and throw your arm up. You're open!

STEP 3: Time your run perfectly – be on the shoulder of the last defender. Don't go too soon or you'll be offside.

STEP 4: Sprint hard! Leave the defender eating your dust. There's no way they can keep up with you!

STEP 5: Aim your run slightly to the side, to open up an angle on goal and tempt the keeper out.

STEP 6: As the keeper comes, chip the ball by digging your foot in under it. With some practise the ball should fly over the goalie, and back down into the net. Wonder goal!

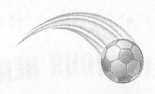

TEST YOUR KNOWLEDGE

1. Which football club did Fran's dad play for?

2. Which famous Arsenal player did Fran look up to when she was a child?

3. What was the name of Fran's coach at The Royals?

4. What is the name of Reading FC's home stadium?

5. What Women's World Cup match from 2007 was Fran watching on the TV?

6. Which Everton player gave her autograph to Fran?

7. Who did Fran play against for her first senior match at Reading FC?

8. Who did The Royals play at The Den?

9. What did Fran study at Bucks University?

10. In which tournament did Fran receive the Player of the Final award?

11. Reading FC Women won the FA Premier League Southern Division in which season?

12. Which team did Fran play against in her senior debut for England?

13. What nickname was Fran given after she scored against Mexico in the Women's World Cup 2015?

14. In which minute did Fran score against Manchester City in the Women's FA Cup semi-final?

Answers below. . . No cheating!

1. *Sunderland AFC* **2.** *Thierry Henry* **3.** *Kelly Chambers* **4.** *Madejski Stadium* **5.** *England v Argentina* **6.** *Jill Scott* **7.** *Doncaster Belles* **8.** *Millwall Lionesses* **9.** *Applied Coaching Science* **10.** *The World University Games* **11.** *2012–13* **12.** *Sweden* **13.** *Mini Messi* **14.** *123rd*